DOLPHINOLOGY

THE 3 YOGAS
OF
THIS DREAM WE CALL LIFE

*how to use inner sonar to
see-feel others' hearts
and wake while dreaming*

DolphinOlogy, Inc.
Los Angeles

DOLPHINOLOGY, INC.

Website: dolphinology.org

Contact: dolphinology@icloud.com

© 2015 DolphinOlogy, Inc. Second Edition Revised

References quotes on Pg. 131 and 196 are from *The Tibetan Book of the Dead: the Great Liberation Through Hearing in the Bardo* by Guru Rinpoche, according to Karma Lingpa, translated with commentary by Francesca Fremantle and Chögyam Trungpa (Shambala Classics, 2003)

Print Version
ISBN #978-1500196271

Also available from DolphinOlogy, Inc.:

Dark Retreat

and coming soon

Solar-Powered Humans:
The Science and Discipline Sun-Gazing

DolphinOlogy

TABLE OF CONTENTS

FOREWORD:
QUESTION
EVERYTHING

Hi, it's DolphinOlogy's founder, remaining nameless as "i" am not sure who i am, but certainly not this body or this identity. And that's the main teaching that we hope to share, experientially, so you will get that the goal of lucid dreaming is NOT to be able to control your dreams, but to get past them, to the Clear Light[1].

DolphinOlogy is an idea to bring the highest teachings for a new era – GENERATION LIBERATION – for those who are past entertainment, and physical fitness, and are catching up with the Asian/Himalayan cultures who actually try not to use the word "I", especially those on the path of awakening as they get deeper in.

This is actually a lucid dream practice: to refer to one's self in the third person. Masters do this. That's why these hands are the typist for the cosmos instead of "I" trying you to sell you

---

1 Clear Light: past the dream state to the primordial "no thing" of bliss and cosmic consciousness.

some dream kits. (We give a version of everything away for free at DolphinOlogy.org.)

Getting past the dream stories and the "I" is the Tibetan Buddhist *Maha Yoga* path... and, well, the goal of the Masters. When no more story exists, one has cleansed their "*Samsāras*[2]". So if you don't like the idea of LIVE, DIE and REPEAT, then getting past the dream is the idea.

However, the only way out of the ballpark, if you're a baseball addict, is to watch the game without excitement. So, too, by waking up inside a dream, one can gently allow it, play with it, and realize the dream characters are all a reflection of the dreamer.

Pet the dream monster with compassion, and it will turn into a friend. This was a vision experienced during twelve days in the dark, written about in *Endless Cosmic Orgasm* (2nd edition renamed as *Dark Retreat*.)

Behind every cloud of drama is blue sky. Tibetan Masters are known as Sky-Gazers, for they practice their lucidity for the day, the dream, and the death *bardo* (in-between state) by looking into the sky past the clouds, past the action in front of them... at the blue sky in their heart.

Keep in mind, this is not a book, it's a research experiment, an exploration/notes to self on the highest teachings found after a near-death experience determined sharing and caring (for self as well as others) was an instant new priority.

So, enjoy, and forgive the insanity, as the near-death experience was a psychosis-inducing *kundalini* crisis/brain-

---

[2] *Samsāras:* past actions that leave impressions, desires, and stories that come back as karma and must find a resolution.

damage trauma from a "Plant Medicine" (Ayahuasca)... meaning what you are about to read is coming through questionable hands.

QUESTION EVERYTHING. Especially whose hands these are. Yours and mine. At your discretion and convenience, please: question everything, and *Feel* How It *Sees*.

*Feelings expressed
are paramount
over words.*

*Love in action
is paramount over justice.*

*Songs sung
are paramount over thoughts*

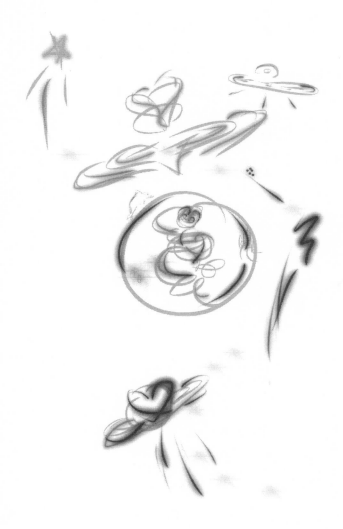

*Viewed from space,
the clearest evidence of
love
on Earth is
Dolphins and Whales.*

1. INTRODUCTION

DolphinOlogy

"I wake from a dream in which I'm a Dolphin, and realize I'm a Dolphin dreaming I'm a man."

- Lao Tsu (re-porpoised)

DREAM YOGIS

Dolphins are the only beings on the planet that naturally remain awake while they sleep. Half of their brain dreams in a R.E.M. state of consciousness; the other half remains awake, with an eye open underwater looking for predators.

The most accomplished Yogis and Tribal Dream Masters can achieve this state when in deep practice, like the solitude they go into before dropping their bodies, (you used to call this "death".)

This makes Dolphins the most conscious beings on the planet, as they don't have to meditate for years to achieve this awakened state. After all, who is closer to God than our friends of the sea?

We have something to learn from them.

THREE YOGAS OF DOLPHINOLOGY

Dolphins use their bodies (in this story that channeled through these hands) to practice telling stories with their imaginations. In other words, their DNA is engineered with the three Dolphin Yogas:

1. *Dolphins dream while awake.* So for them, life is a play of building the muscle of loving imagination, and the sharing of the communal dream. Dolphins are the ultimate village of love, which is why pods join in massive numbers with the same love song chants of oneness.

2. *Dolphins communicate with feeling-pictures (echolocation.)* Without words to get caught in their own stories ("headgames") they are able to ping and reflect sound to see-feel the expansion or contraction of hearts and breathing rates in the beings around them, thus they are always present to love, or cries for love.

3. *Dolphins have no hands to build or destroy, only a mouth to deal with one thing at a time.* They naturally release everything back into the dream, so they are free to love, free of attachment, and able to let go. Because, as they know, life dissolves back into the source: everything is let go of eventually. And the purpose is to work on awakening.

By practicing these three Dolphin yogas, you can write your own *DolphinOlogy* answers to life questions.

CONSCIOUS BREATHERS
Dolphins are also conscious breathers who know that when they have completely awakened and liberated their human brothers and sisters, they will be extracted back to the "mother ship."

"Ah," you say, *"Science-fiction,"*… well let's go on a Dolphin-Alien adventure!

Imagine high spirits are thrown into Dolphin bodies and extracted back when they have built up the muscle of their imaginations to serve on the "Council of Creation" that builds a new planet through holographic nano-tech visioning. Cool concept, right? Perhaps these are the other realms on the way to the NO-THING (*Wu Chi* in Taoism) from which perhaps we came…

The Dolphin references are just a fun way to communicate it all, along with some true science, in this brief dream we share.

So, the three qualities of the Dolphin are echoed in their natural laws: **Release, Feel, Dream**. RFD.

DREAM-SHARING INSTEAD OF TEXTING
1. Love in action Releases the need for justice. Because there are only two emotions: love, and cries for love. Therefore anybody who seemingly misbehaves just needs to have a higher "porpoise" to work towards. A grander perspective on the mission for their life.

Dream-Sharing helps build this spiritual mission with letters from the Source. The Talmud says a dream unexamined is like an unopened letter from God.

Everyone has an inner Dolphin-Buddha nature that is flowering at its own speed. It's our genetic/spiritual imprint to help all beings liberate towards this, and it's easy and fun with DolphinOlogy – and please form your own faith when you come up with something hipper, cooler, wetter.

2. Feelings expressed are paramount over words. Love is better expressed through action than by texting.

3. Sharing Dreams releases stories and builds the Dolphin pod (tribe) toward light, toward the imaginal muscle that stories are the creators (awareness that our stories equal our unconscious mythologies that are the blueprints of our possibilities.)

Dreaming also builds the muscle of lucidity (awareness that the dreamer is dreaming) so that the highest practitioners may serve on the Council of Creation when extracted back to the mother* ship.

* Buddhists refer to mother as the eternal void from which we all came. The vast expanse of sky. The source of all. Envision your own mother ship (walk on board to discover what this

means) and treat all beings who've come to experience this love life as your mother in thousands of lifetimes previous. Hopefully, if you join the Dolphin pod, you may sing with DolphinOlogists everywhere, for...

The main spiritual practice of Dolphins (and whales,) besides dreaming, is singing.

Songs sung are paramount over thoughts.

Every faith teaches that chanting brings one closer to the Creator... and all elements have a resonant hum. This sound for the cosmos is much like the sacred "AUM" (pronounced "OMMMM".) Science has measured it, so you can Google the frequency.

This book is practical and not filled with useless facts, so if you don't understand something just try it out and if it feels right, you are on your way.

In the same way that sand forms into geometric shapes (mandalas) when you hit certain notes and put sand on top of a speaker, for example, the universe forms patterns from sounds. Sanscrit, the ancient alphabet, was formed in just this way. Look at the leaves, or your children, and see the fractal geometry repeating in patterns.

We are each holographic[3] fractals riding on sound waves, repeating on waves of attention and imagination... from the very first sound of the cosmos. *"First was the word."*

No surprise that Dolphin vocalizations (echolocation or sonar) as has been recorded by the "cymaglyph" (a photo on a water cell) reveals a holographic fractal image. It's official because science says so, LOL.

---

[3] Holographic: one fragment contains the whole.

Anyway, lets move on heart feeling for the rest of this book. The heart feeling of sacred songs (or chants, known as Mantras) carries fractals, which disrupt patterns of thought and ignite inner realms to bring us back to cosmic consciousness.

Mantra in many faiths, with enough devotion, can release *kundalini*[4], the creative fire that activates and levitates meditators, and releases the nectar that allows Yogis (and Dolphins and Whales) to remain in the breathless state, drawing life energy from the elements. *Kundalini* awakening results in the whole brain being activated, allowing the full human potential to be explored.

Let's get our inner Dolphin on...

---

[4] *Kundalini*: the life force experienced as orgasm. When released by Dolphins or Yogis it's experienced as whole-body spiritual orgasm.

DolphinOlogy

2. THE PORPOISE OF LIFE

Be sure to join DolphinOlogists by writing all over this book the moment you have any inspiration, thought to work out, or feeling-picture appearing on the farthest ocean of your imagination. We started the process out for you...

Your inner
Buddha-Dolphin
knows

To become aware you are dreaming while you are living...

and living while you are dreaming.

To be lucid in your dreams and lucid in your life...[5]

- so you can manifest,

- move to the next level of consciousness,

- and liberate yourself from suffering on the Earth plane.

LUCK: *the clarity to attract similar consciousness, and the presence of mind to act on inspiration.*

---

[5] Lucidity: the ability to be aware while dreaming, and the ability to feel your dreams (be conscious) while awake.

What is your definition of "LUCK"?

and a quiet mind is like a dark country setting to watch the stars

Just like a star field visible at night cannot be seen during the day, or in a city full of lights, we are constantly in a "dream" of wish-fulfilling.

& finding our destiny

We are shooting stars of possibility.

Becoming aware of our thoughts - so that we can be awake to our dreams and creative potential - allows us to see possibilities, and thereby attract similar consciousness to help us manifest those possibilities into reality.

CREATION

- A story...

Life begins in lucid dreams.

In space, trade is controlled by a Council of the greatest imaginations. After many lifetimes of play and building the muscle of lucid imagination, the highest dolphin-Yogis are extracted back to the mother ship to work on this CGI[6].

---

[6] CGI means "Council of Greatest Imaginations". Humans have tapped into the intelligence-sonar field and are beginning to develop their own early version, where CGI stands for "Computer Generated Imagery".

What is your definition of
"SYNCHRONICITY"?

Oh! credit
Deepak Chopra
w/ the stars
metaphor
read his
"synchrodestiny"

As technology develops and integrates with life forms, humans will have re-engineered themselves as smaller versions of the cosmic creator.

(Don't take any of this, or anything, literally. For all is a play of light expressing through games.)

But do allow it to be a guide. Especially allow *yourself* to be your *own* guide.

Do not pit man against Dolphin, or fish against computer. All is one.

So, in space, these greatest imaginations get to run the universe, because they have such developed dreaming capacity that they can create worlds.

They use a nano-technological creation device to "terraform" new worlds.

TERRAFORM: *to populate with flora and fauna – to birth a living eco-system.*

In other words: images, stories and feelings go in; Nature comes out.

How would you build CREATION?

✓ through
Love, Song & Surf
✓ w/a way back to the light ♡

DOLPHIN NANOTECHNOLOGY

When civilizations need to create life on new planets, the Council lucidly joins imaginations and feeds the reality printer. Lets call it a Story Translator.

Lucidity is key.

This would seem to be the definition of Higher Consciousness.

LUCIDIAN: a being with well-developed lucidity.

When the council LUCIDLY joins imaginations, it's important to note that sound waves carry everywhere in water, and the waves blend in a harmony. Whales sing to dolphins, Nature drums with rain, and thunder sometimes provides a bass drum.

"Lucidly joining in imagination" means the Council is awake (lucid) to the harmony of all creation, and TO what is in the highest interest to take it on a cycle of play from dark to light and back again.

So, "all creation is one" means we are becoming emotionally in synch, through the waves of our body and the stilling of our mind, to be descended upon by the universal consciousness (what many call GOD.) Is this what "Grace" is? Perhaps. So I ask you...

What is your definition of "HIGHER CONSCIOUSNESS"?

✓ humility

✓ Surrender

This act of circuits knows nothing

LOVE LETTERS EVERYWHERE, WHEN YOU RELEASE YOUR INNER POET
The introduction of a "High Council" is merely wordplay to create more METAPHOR for our highest Selves.

This book gets into outlandish metaphor; all is true as it resonates with your heart's joy (who you really are - a giggling Dolphin baby.) So, remember, you are a member of the Highest Council... here to remember your Self.

HOW DOLPHINS WEIGH TRUTH
Dolphins weigh truth by how much it makes their hearts expand.

Nothing is true in this book except to the degree that your Inner Dolphin7 tells you the ocean of the heart is warm, still, and blossoming with rays of sunshine.

Example: *Did he cheat on you or did she break your trust? Does it make your heart expand, even if you saw it happen?*

The TRUTH is that the universe seeks your compassion and allowance for the underlying STORY, as you were the story creator. So feel this: you are a self-repairing story machine, and only going inside with truth will repair the story for the NEXT DREAM.

What is your Story?
? Life is a dream, and on the other side is reality - use this time wisely to release ego and join love.

---

7 Inner Dolphin: your I.D., idea, identity.

3. TRUE BEINGS OF EARTH

WHERE DO DOLPHINS COME FROM?

In order to build the "muscle" of lucidity, the Council of Imaginations DNA-engineered beings with:

A) No hands but sensuous skin, so they cannot build or destroy, but mainly make lots of love.

B) A language based on images, so they cannot interpret words. Instead they have visual sonar that can vibrate images and see feelings by looking into the body tensions of fellow Dolphins.

C) The ability to "split" the brain to be consciously aware while dreaming; to be in an R.E.M. state while awake.

These beings are what we know as Dolphins and Whales.

EARTH LEASE

Earth was created to house Dolphins and Whales in its oceans. The land animals were created to give play to the Imaginations and let the unifying force of loving dreamers cycle into higher and higher consciousness.

Grand Operating System

What is your definition of "GOOD ORDERLY DIRECTION"?

Of **"GOD"?**

Love

Of **"HIGH COUNCIL"?**

COUNCIL OF IMAGINATIONS
Long ago, Earth was leased to the Council of Highest Imaginations (CHI,) who implanted their greatest dreamers into the bodies of these Dolphins for a lifetime of play in Earth's oceans, in order to exercise the muscles of lucid dreaming and storytelling.

HIGH MINDS
Many Dolphins propagated from the original Council members. But still, among the millions of Dolphins on Earth, there remains a rotating core of high minds that are extracted back to the home planet to train further, to be ready to take their place on future councils.

COSMIC CONSCIOUSNESS
What Carl Jung refers to as "mythological archetypes" and the "cosmic unconscious" is literally powered by the very high minds that travel beneath the surface of the oceans.

GRAND OPERATING DESIGNER
The Creation Device is what many refer to as GOD: information and hopes go in; life comes out. Thoughts are regenerated holographically, meaning that each individual thought is available to all.

WHAT IS PRAYER? WHAT IS HUMAN?
The more passionate and lucid and true the thought, the more it reflects back to the thinker. Man calls this prayer.

In fact, man's creation of computers is simply his duplicating early versions of himself, in the hope of recreating the Source of all.

How would you prepare to make yourself of service to a Council of HIGH BEINGS?

c vegetarian diet
c not hurt others or self
c kindness
c only eat from the garden
c lead by example
c protect animals and
humans who have
forgotten thier true nature.

WITNESS CONSCIOUSNESS

Whatever the play of Grand Operating Design, we are left with this important constant: *The Witness* (let's call it *Dolphin Consciousness.*)

THE POWER OF N.O.W.

We can experience The Witness, NOW[8], by simply asking *"Who is reading this book?"* and *"Who is the thinker behind the eyes which read these words?"*

This Witness is our light-body traveling companion. This consciousness existed before and will exist after, according to the ancient texts, and the tribes with no texts.

The True Beings of Earth, Dolphins and Whales, can be our inspiration, as we who have stilled our minds will travel with the True Beings back to the light-body dimension.

To join the True Being-ness, take a look at the world:

FOUR NOBLE DOLPHIN TRUTHS

1. Recognize the beauty and drama and illusion that veil the cycle of birth, aging, disease and death.

2. Devote to self and others the practice of integrating with The Witness (Dolphin Consciousness.)

3. Recognize others as Self; the same Witness lives through the eyes and consciousness of all beings.

4. Connect with the Earth, which also has that same consciousness, and surrender to help all life move towards oneness. Lets call it "Yoga" (to yoke into one) or "Love."

---

[8] NOW: Naturally Organized Wow!

Would

What makes you HUMAN?

If you were a Dolphin?

helping others
meditate
get off sugar,
dairy, flour
& share Dreams

Yoga-ing into one; One Love.
This is what Dolphins do. Feel their smile.
Know-feel this truth.

So, with this muscle of The Witness, we will increase our Dolphin merit (karma,) and the muscle of imagination, and our release of "story" will bring us closer to homecoming.

YIN/YANG

If "building the muscle of imagination" and "release of story" seem to contradict each other, remember, that is the play of yin/yang, light and dark. A Dolphin can only have what he is willing to toss away. With one mouth to hold onto something, he can't have it again until he releases it.

ATLANTEANS

The lost continent of Atlantis[9] worshipped and worked with Dolphins to achieve higher consciousness. Atlanteans were artists and dreamers whose technology eventually separated the people from Nature. Just as nuclear power challenges Earth leaders to wake up, Atlantis' technology ended their civilization.

And, as history repeats itself, (since our true history is that we are spirits playing in a physical realm,) reclaiming that muscle to wake up into our Witness Consciousness becomes the one thing we can do, for ourselves and for each other, that will resonate for eons.

---

[9] Atlantis: the seaside civilization referred to by Greek Philosopher's like Pythagoras, inventor of the musical scale, and Plato. Source: Wikipedia.

QUIET THE MIND
Recently, Navy sonar has interrupted the sole purpose of Dolphins and Whales, who are here to share their stories with each other, and with the earthbound version of the "Creation Device." This has resulted in what is experienced as weather phenomena and mass shifts in consciousness.

ORGANIC COMPUTERS: HUMANS?
Eons ago, the bringers of life to the universe created organic computers: humans, who now recognize the need to recreate life.

So, the Navy's use of sonar is primarily, like all instruments of war, man playing with rebuilding his ability to sense, create, and control his reality.

However, by interrupting dolphin and whale communications, our use of sonar interferes with the flow of life to the very beings responsible for Earth's balance.

Wouldn't it make sense, as we place noise pollution in the water of high mind-dreamers, that noise will be created in Nature?

And in the further play of consciousness, as we deplete our resources, imagination will continue to give play to reality. So perhaps:

If humans are ever taken over by aliens, it will be because Earth is subject to invasion by Alien strip miners.

Of course, this is all the extraction of an instinct, or dream, or creative exercise that played through this writer's imagination...

Perhaps Monsanto, Tepco (Fukushima,) General Electric are the aliens strip-mining the Earth.

YOUR INNER ALIEN / HUG
What works for you is what is important. Your inner Alien may decide to mine the love in your heart. So let's create some excess love. I give you a big hug, just by sending these words. Feel it. That's what makes this writer into a Dolphin for this brief moment. HUG YOU.

BEYOND DRAMA
And wouldn't it make sense that, to the degree our minds are still caught in un-stillness, in story, in karmic seeds of light and dark; then *that* consciousness will travel to a dimension just as thick as that story; just as grasping as those karmic seeds.

> **KARMIC SEEDS: Past actions that create guilt, longing and drama that will put expectation and attempted resolution into play in the future. Expectation creates results. Repetition of childhood survival tactics into adult relationships, ex. dating Daddy or Mommy.**
>
> (When watching people slip into past-life death scenarios, they often have birthmarks where they recount having been fatally wounded.)

If we liberate past the cycle of birth and death, then what would the DolphinOlogist-poet inside you say The Witness is like?

A drop of water in the ocean? An atom of love inside the universal heart? A mini-Buddha, in a field of Buddhas, in the universal willingness that breathes for eternity? The Clear Light of the sky behind the clouds?

GENERATION SILENCE

Silence is the next generation. Smiles and hugs will communicate more than the old-human need for drama-news. Silent retreats, if you haven't heard about them, liberate humans from story and stress. They are getting popular in yoga circles. Check some out on Google. Or join us for one at DolphinOlogy.org.

KUNDALINI YOGIS OF THE OCEAN

When a Dolphin leaps from the water in the wild, (isn't it great that all your activism has ended the enslavement of Dolphins at parks like *Sea World* and *Atlantis-Feel The Future*?) isn't it an intuitive download that it is experiencing Kundalini, Seiki, Chi, the Holy Ghost, the universal life force that makes the Kalahari Bushmen shiver and laugh with a beyond-erotic ecstasy before they astral travel to the Source?

50,000 YEAR-OLD BUSHMEN LAUGH AT US

It's not a secret. Of course, as I learned from Dr. Bradford Keeney10, the Kalahari Bushmen laugh that modern culture thinks it can learn spirituality from reading or using words, or sitting still and meditating. They believe you laugh and tease and shake-dance, and then the Spirit teaches you, carrying you away on the current of electricity that yogis prepare for carefully, so as not to go insane when the "kundalini serpent" is released.

---

10 *The Bushmen Way of Tracking God* by Bradford Keeney PhD, shakingmedicine.com

DREAMTIME TRIBES

To find the next lineage after Dolphins, one would only have to follow the dreamtime tribes... often worshippers of Dolphins.

Hailing from the original birthplace of humans (according to scientific genetic tracking,) it seems the Bushmen enjoy the same laughter and play as a path to the Divine that Dolphins do.

With perfect synchro-destiny, in his book *The Bushmen Way of Tracking God*, Dr. Keeney describes how the Bushmen are transported to a dreamlike place where the mystery school begins. Dream prophecies are central to the culture. These Dolphins of the African desert welcomed Dr. Keeney when he showed up in their camp. They dreamt of him the night before.

Teaching, as Guru Singh taught this DolphinOlogist, allows a portal of higher downloads to come into the teacher to fulfill his momentum.

GO TO MYSTERY SCHOOL

If you can get rid of thoughts altogether, step on to the great mother at the birthplace of humanity, uncoil the Kundalini serpent, let the lotus flower blossom, release the rope of God, the Divine river of life-force - we can let laughter and shaking love overtake us and send us to the great Mystery School.

The key is to take a first step. Here is a one-breath exercise to try:

STOP.

Don't breathe until your body breathes for you.

What does it feel like to be breathed for by the Grand Operating Designer?

4. IF SPIRITUALITY WERE A DOLPHIN'S DREAM

Here is the information downloaded as the next step in society's movement toward an elevated consciousness.

All of these movements will have a common denominator: feelings over intellect.

GENERATION LIBERATION
• "Generation Liberation" will result from Fukushima. The young artists and yogis will realize that becoming enlightened is the only way to save the planet and ease the suffering of souls.

• Indigo children will appear who will have vivid and lucid dreams, intuition and connection with each other. These children will recall past lives and will be channels of instructional downloads for the reshaping of society.

• Relationships will be under tremendous pressure as struggles for control give way to the sharing of feelings. Village life will become necessary to support life long partnerships.

• Politics will give way to an Internet-based democracy. Online activism will determine the future of the planet, as corporate control of government policies will be overturned by sites like avaaz.org.

TAKE ONLY WHAT YOU NEED

• Economics will move toward a time-barter system. Village economics will replace failing banking policies, which are based on *take more than you need,* a system that is not in congruence with the gentleman farmer.

The gentleman farmer picks food for dinner, and doesn't hoard food to sell. The closer we grow toward this original practice of the native land, the closer we grow toward connection with the Earth and ourselves. And then you can barter for variety instead of flirting in the aisles of Whole Foods.

• A movement toward participation in the healing arts will adjust consumerism's effect of emotional medication. We can already see this in the replacement of Western medicine with the preventative healing arts.

ORGANIC
Cancer will become so unacceptable that organic food becomes mandatory and meat-eating* is equated with disease. Foods labeled "ORGANIC," which title was bought by the FDA, will be replaced by "TRUE ORGANIC" or something like that.

* VEGETARIANS IN SPIRIT
Dolphins are vegetarians in spirit - they don't take more than they need from the fish tree, and they use SONAR to stun the fish they eat thereby vibrating the little soul out of the fish body, liberating it with *Kundalini* (what you know in a small way as orgasm,) before biting into it. Eat me God.

So for anyone looking for contrasts in this book, look for metaphors, and if you are a fisherman or a meat-eater looking to feel good, please use your mouth to catch fish after making love to it; no trawling nets or factory farming or antibiotics to fatten the fish up and then sell it to unsuspecting humans.

What will happen to EARTH as our population grows?

importance of liberating
from the cycle of birth,
drama, disease and death
in physical form will lead people
to meditate and old school yoga

END TIMES/ NEW TIMES

What are considered the "end times," but are truly a call for change, will occur for the benefit of all, and will look like this:

• Dolphins and whales have already begun committing mass suicide by beaching themselves. You can sign online petitions against Navy Sonar at DolphinOlogy.org.

• Protests will start where humans confront other humans on their inhumane treatment and slaughter of Dolphins and whales.

• Because the members of the High Council of Imagination (let's call them "Lucidians") are not fully physical beings, and are composed more of light than of solid matter, they will communicate their mission to rid the oceans of sonar by transmitting instructional dreams to certain children and those receptive to lucidity.

How do you justify bringing children into this world of SUFFERING and JOY?

(Especially when there are children without families available for adoption?)

FLYING SAUCERS APPEAR

As the dreams of children cause conflict and protest, eventually the appearance of oceanic atmospheric phenomena will signal the Council's first effort at removing their high beings from the Oceans.

BOTTLED-NOSE DOLPHIN WATER

A hostile group of Aliens may appear who will be surveying Earth's oceans for minerals. Bodies of water may be vaporized and the oceans may find themselves subject to chemically altering phenomena.

NOTE: Whatever portion of this book you would like to interpret metaphorically, please do so (as with the book of your own life.) Therefore hostile Aliens may be nothing more than less-than-helpful thoughts of our own minds.

And since the roaring thunders and demons that can appear in the visions after death, in the Buddhist scriptures, are nothing more than the play of our own minds, it would be good to go meditate after you finish reading this today.

5. DOLPHINOLOGY: THE POWER OF THE LUCID MIND

"Most people live on the surface of life. But it is by deep-sea diving in the ocean of thought that you receive the pearls of knowledge."

- Pramahansa Yogananda

LUCID: awareness with the qualities of a neutral witness, so one's clarity isn't shaken or lost by grasping, or avoidance, or fascination.

LUCID DREAMS
Lucid dreaming is a core teaching of *DolphinOlogy*.

When one is lucid in life, one becomes more apt to be lucid in dream, which is far more difficult, because a dream is a constant stream of karmic seeds coming at the witness of the dream.

And when two dream lucidly together, creation becomes exponential.

This phenomenon is particular to the core Council of High Beings and to certain sects of Bön Buddhists, who practice lucid dreaming in order to die consciously. *As you fare in dreams you shall fare in death.*

Other Earth groups have been known to pursue this liberation goal as well. These are the most powerful minds on the planet.

Many inventors have tapped into the ability to have lucid dreams. James Cameron credits lucid dreaming with the inspiration behind AVATAR. The sewing machine was invented in a lucid dream. Paul McCartney, Beethoven, and many prolific artists have brought music from the dream state.

TESTS TO WAKE UP
The ultimate test every night is whether we can liberate from our stories and suffering, to "wake up."

59

Doesn't the fact that we all sleep at night seems to be the great metaphor of life? EVERY NIGHT IS A CHANCE TO GO INTO THE DARKNESS ...into the practice of dying. Dying to the day. Dying to the waking life.

Perhaps the purpose of our dense, pain-collecting bodies is to provide a gymnasium for the mind... whereby the reactive mind can be replaced with Conscious Creation. Anger and fear are replaced with the feeling of love. Negativity is dissolved by the excitement of possibility, of creation: remembering that you are the Creator.

To love...

To serve...

To remember...

LUCID LIVING: *the action of remembering and acting on your Oneness, your creativity.*

GET PAST THE STORY MACHINE
But remember, the true goal is to get past the story machine. It's not really about the dream or cool experiences. Dreams are a test, coming faster than the seeds of karma do during the day, so you might want to get past them. Lucid dreaming is a great practice ground for Liberation.

What is the great METAPHOR of life to you?

What is the "way out" to you?

non-reactivity
to become the sky
- allow the clouds to pass
knowing we are the
Reflection of stillness
in the ocean of our soul

ALL ONE-MIND UNITY

I have lived
I have dreamed
All of these lives

Why have I not died
For I am
Not born
Again

I am you
In the sky

Until blazing,
I see
I know
I feel

Excerpted from "The Great Sayings" of the *Upanishads*: *Tat Tvam Asi* (Thou art that) and *Ahum Brahmasmi* (I am Divine.)

LEGGO MY EGO
Do Dolphins have Ego?

Perhaps, as they too have to survive a physical i-dent-ity. Notice the "dent" in "i"dent-ity... or the breast reference in the same word. These are word puns for those prone to silly wastes of time, like the Ego writing these words. Please help me surrender from anything that takes away from time preparing for merging with the Divine.

Would you play word games, or get a job, if you just woke up in a lucid dream?

Or would we extend that time to merge with the dream characters who are all us, and then dream in HD the Divine bliss of the all-potentiality instead of human form?

This thought occurred, last night, after a weekend of Oregon's Peace Festival, where dancing led to a heart-opening play of arms moving in girly fashion toward the stage... After 50 years of hip dancing, the body was now shedding tears realizing how controlled the shoulders and heart have been, both in dance and in life. Thank you Goddesses of Dance!

The thought occurred: *Since dream scenarios move by at the speed of light, what happens when we die?* If no form can affix and we do merge with the all-light, then it is imperative to practice looking for this clear light in the day. Is this not true?

MERGE MERGE MERGE
Look for the brightest spot, don't even move the eyes to it, and immediately feel, *DIVINE LORD, COSMIC LIGHT, G_D, AAAAAAAAAAH, MERGE MERGE MERGE....*

Wouldn't it be great to look into the cosmos of the eye, into the darkness of the pupil, and feel, *AAAAAH, this is where the light comes from, from the void…?*

Refining the games of spiritual perception, does this not feel right? Does this preoccupation with spiritual perception games, feel like the past-time of a master? Or does the master say, "Hello, old friend," to all thoughts, and then simply feel Prana/life force tingle through the space?

So, can ego be thought of just like the constriction of muscles to protect the space of the heart? Is ego like an egg? Do we form a hard shell to protect against potential egg-crackers? How can an egg-cracker be spiritual development?

Perhaps that is best *"answered by the poet responsible,"* – if "i" remember right – from the MATRIX movies. Regardless, Tellhard Jardin, said, "The True self grows in inverse proportion to the ego."

Dr. Jim Hardt, who studies the ability of the brain to go into alpha state, says the big blocks are the ability to forgive, which is controlled by the 5 Hindrances (and #6 he just discovered):

1. DOUBT

2. DROWSINESS

3. DISTRACTABILITY

4. BOREDOM

5. AVERSION (any form of ILL WILL)

6. FORGETFULNESS

Good ones to look at, when the opportunity arises to pick growth over patterns and the "real world" (lol.)

6. DOLPHIN LOVE & COMMUNICATION

Sonar allows a Dolphin to see the constriction of musculature of other Dolphins.

Constriction of breath and musculature is what also happens to humans when they think negative thoughts or have negative feelings. This body armoring holds memories and creates patterns.

FEELING-SONGS... BEYOND WORDS

Evolution has taken Dolphins, our more advanced Lucidian selves, and done away with the need for words.

We would be wise in times of conflict to adhere to this same approach, and instead of reacting, breathe, empathize, and simply emit a sound to resonate with a friend who appears to be under the influence of a negative feeling or experience.

THE DOLPHIN ART OF "I FEEL..."

To contact and connect heart-to-heart might be more natural or comfortable with a love, but even with friends and colleagues, it is a wonderful practice to duplicate this Dolphin behavior of breathing and holding space. Then, and only then, becoming lucid enough to see that what they are going through is a dream, one should then express feelings without blame or judgment: *"I feel x-y-z..."* Practice with, *"I feel uncomfortable..."*

WHY DOLPHINS HAVE NO CONFLICT

Words are controlled and manipulative, and even with the best of intentions, they contain subtext, which can be sexy and fun, and a lure into many a compulsive game.

But words pale in comparison with simply breathing into your feelings and being present to what is being felt by the other person in the conflict.

YOUR SONAR

Dolphins sonar ping those they are in conflict with. This is how a Dolphin will read the body tensions of the other Dolphin and be able to empathize.

We too have this ability, though it may seem less obvious and direct. Have you ever felt the vibe shift? That is your "sonar" working. Trust it.

CONFLICT

Conflict is often the result of information outside the current situation. A conscious or unconscious memory of a past event being re-stimulated, a reference from an outside bit of information, or something somebody else said.

Find the outside or inside source of story and be free of conflict. Stop using words; use poetic feelings that look for the compassion in each moment, and become more free.

Some of my favorite ways to eliminate circuits that feed old stories:

• Tapping or Emotional Freedom Technique (E.F.T.) See *Chapter 9: Dolphin Practices*.

• Dolphin DeHypnosis, see DolphinOlogy.org.

• Meditation (search YouTube for Deepak Chopra's great online teachings.)

CLOSE YOUR EYES

GO INSIDE

WATCH THOUGHTS RISE

LET THEM GLIDE

TO THE SURFACE

AND POP!

When one breathes and becomes attuned to how one feels, and puts these qualities into the words one speaks, the effect is transcendent.

ↄ Yoga
ↄ being in nature
ↄ listening to trees

What is your favorite way to stop REACTIVITY?

ↄ tapping / E.F.T.
ↄ dolphin therapy
ↄ experiencing the day as a dream

GAMES

Games are mostly compulsive on Earth, broken up by humor and presence and lucidity and lovemaking: qualities and abilities that Dolphins are wonderful at.

VOLUNTARY GAMES

Voluntary games mean that we are not caught in the drama of winning, and can bounce in and out without attachment to the outcome.

COMPULSIVE GAMES

Compulsive games are ones that become more and more serious, until we lose track of the fact that we are enjoying the push-pull of the relationships involved.

Compulsive games include rescue and betrayal and "fixing," or seeking revenge for wrongs.

To be lucid, we must master the voluntary self-aware game-state.

Like a human mind, but to a far greater degree, the Dolphin mind creates images and feelings that direct the dream.

NO MORE DRAMA

Because the Dolphin is also awake while dreaming, it can direct its own dreaming mind, and its dream "character," to situations that allow for voluntary games... meaning the attention continues to turn towards stories that don't push the Dolphin imagination to get compulsively caught in drama.

When these stories are spun in the dreamscape, and the Dolphin forgets it's a dream, it may no longer be present to the other side of the brain that is monitoring its half-sleeping body, on watch for breath, or food, or its beloved, or predators... adjusted to remain awake and aware even while the Dolphin is dreaming.

How do you admit to your own INSANITY?

I love to you
♡
How did we get here?

LOVERS

No matter what kind of lover one is challenged with, unless that lover is a high-practicing DolphinOlogist or other kind of lucid dreamer, one must remember that they're dealing with a person who is referring to "mind."

NO MORE CRAZY LOVE

A mind that cannot witness itself, that is mainly a collection of circuits formed from past moments of trauma and survival, is inherently crazy. Mind itself is always crazy, unless one can witness it from a distance.

OUR LOVER'S DREAM

So if we can be like a Dolphin, who can split his brain into two awareness units (witness itself) and recall during times of high stress that what we're experiencing is often just re-stimulated past circuitry playing out as current dramas, then we can bring ourselves into our Dolphin nature, avoid identifying with our lover's mind, and allow the re-stimulated abandonment issues to play out as if watching our lover's dream.

Remember, a Dolphin can always sonar its lover's organs and see-feel where there is anger, tension, fear.

vc - not until the other ~~to~~ has the freedom to be right, can they admit te wrongness

When caught up in an un-witnessed dream, the human cannot see him- or herself, nor be reminded by other humans that he or she is unconsciously spinning a story.

In the case of your lover, when the dream/story has played out, then you can re-enter and converse with your lover's spirit instead of his or her insanity.

DOLPHINS DISTANCE CRAZY LOVE
A love's past experiences, limiting beliefs or trauma can easily be re-stimulated. And the individual who is easily triggered may have gone through so much, that his or her tone and attitude will pass from grief to fear to anger to sarcasm. Only then can the humor of the situation be absorbed and witnessed from a distance.

HOW DOES THAT MAKE YOU FEEL?
Since Dolphins use sonar to feel the constriction of their lovers' organs, we can mimic this skill by asking, "*How does that make you feel?*" and your lover will tell about his or her internal state and witness it for him or herself.

See also *Chapter 10: DolphinOlogy for Kids and Parents*: **"BEING HEARD/GETTING NEEDS MET"**.

What would your dream of LOVE be, if you were a Dolphin?

Surfing Waves of Compassion

JOKE – FIGHT – DOLPHIN MAKE-UP SEX

Upon detailing how they feel, if you ask again, *"How does THAT make you feel?"* you will watch them, upon each consecutive pass, rise along the stages of loss as they witness their own mind. Then you can make a joke, make love, or fight it out… recognizing the drama for the insanity it is.

You will have become a Dolphin, perpetually smiling, because you maintain dual states of mind and dream.

✓ teach surfing

If you were a Dolphin, what ways could you MAKE LOVE, other than Dolphin sex or caressing?

✓ gifting anonymously
✓ feeling someone happy
✓ becoming a better healer/teacher

THE DOLPHINOLOGY HANDSHAKE

This beautiful Mantra is a LUCID DREAM ACTIVATOR and DOLPHIN-CONSCIOUSNESS BUILDER. The DolphinOlogy hand-shake also makes humans smile like Dolphins.

IF YOU SHARE IT TEN TIMES, IT ACTIVATES A SURPRISE.

Please share your surprises with us at DolphinOlogy.org on Facebook, Instagram, Twitter or whatever is next: psychic connection, Dolphin sonar inspired by the radiation of Fukushima and cell phones. All is good for in the end it is one: Love.

Okay, DOLPHINOLOGY HANDSHAKE:

Step 1. Say, *"Just a dream,"* and pop fists, bounce back into explosion of light, fingers dancing in the sky.

Or, for more lovemaking, touch the palms of the hands and drift back slowly...

Step 2. Turn the palm to do a palm lucidity check, dream/reality check; is the palm swirling? Who is the witness?

Step 3. Touch the palm to the heart and feel the reflection in the other.

Step 4. Bow forward with love-oneness and say, *"DolphinOlogy."*

If you want to join the Hawaiian tradition, and African tribal traditions, TOUCH FOREHEADS before saying, *"DolphinOlogy."*

How can you truly
FEEL
another as yourself?

7. IF DOLPHINS CREATED THERAPY

Dolphins and Yogis
will be leading
humans into
group love consciousness

If Dolphins created therapy, they might start with their point of view, which is that the body is a game that creates amnesia when YOU (your inner Dolphin) download into it. And since the porpoise is to remember your way back out (back to love,) the body helps by collecting trauma and loss: because when loss builds enough, it explodes into tears and you have a window back to your true nature. This is why babies can laugh and cry in the same instant.

But this culture, unlike Dolphin communities, accumulates too many losses too quickly, and we don't have enough ritual or tears to keep up.

SO! If you are NOT YET a BABY or a DOLPHIN...

IF:

- Nightmares? Can't sleep?

- Lover left you crippled by pain?

- Sad or Angry or Addicted to something?

- Psychotic from psychedelics?

- Filling yourself up with shopping or eating or just FEELING OVERWHELMED?

- Mom or Dad still pushing buttons? (Cause they installed them.)

- Doctors got you supporting the synthetic Armageddon of drug companies by labeling your circuits as ADD, ADHD, OCD, XYZ, ZZZ?

KNOW THIS: You are perfect. The circuits that learn to shut you down by protecting your body from pain, or reminders of past pain, sometimes add up. These have to be repeatedly dissolved by replaying them; otherwise you go unconscious again to the degree you are re-stimulated by the old trauma.

DOLPHINS DIVE DEEP TO CURE DEPRESSION
Whatever is not replayed (retold while in R.E.M.[11], with your eyes closed, so you are discharging the circuitry,) to the point of laughter, controls you in depression and compulsion. This means you re-dramatize whatever the original trauma is, again and again, crying, then screaming, then being annoyed at doing the exercise, then laughing at the time your brother shoved a crayon in your nose, and stuff even more challenging than that.

METHODS OF TRAUMA RELEASE
A very effective method of "Dolphin De-bugging" is to get the muscle memory to release tension associated with these memories.

There are a few ways we know of:

A. Internal stillness, like meditation, which can take a while if it's a severe trauma.

B. Activating the stored trauma to release through Emotional Freedom Technique (E.F.T.,) which involves tapping acupressure points with your own fingers. This is easy to apply and only requires a Google search for "tapping bulimia", "tapping breakup," etc. See also *Chapter 9: Dolphin Practices.*

---

[11] See *Chapter 11: Dolphin Meditation, TEN-SECOND DOLPHIN CONSCIOUSNESS* for an easy technique for getting into R.E.M. (rapid-eye movement state) while awake.

C. For really deep depression and other wounds, have someone else push you through the pain until it cries out through the stages of resolve: shock, grief, anger, sarcasm, indifference, humor, love.

So, the most powerful way out of deep Dolphin poo, is to have someone else drive you back into your pain-body memories, and who won't let your pain-body say, *"Enough already."*

DOLPHINS DON'T HAVE SHRINKS

Do NOT go to psychiatrists, as they medicate you as a primary tool; thereby pouring oil on circuits and getting them to spread the re-stimulation over the entire neural network, so that it is temporarily lessened and may explode later. Even if a psychiatrist was hip enough to run de-hypnotizing re-dramatizations on you, psychologists do way too much talking, are expensive, and spread the work out over time.

With Dolphin de-hypnosis, one can enter from a spiritual standpoint and work with a friend who has a few simple steps to follow. Much safer, cheaper, faster and easier.

The very act of remembering a trauma knocks people into the same unconsciousness that was necessary to survive it in the first place. So without a guide, this radical spiritual Dolphin technique can make you fall into sleep.

WHEN DOLPHIN YOGA IS NOT ENOUGH

Dolphins might recommend this technique when meditation and Dolphin Yoga, or Emotional Freedom Technique won't do the job:

Dolphin De-Hypnotic Circuit Reduction[12]

Link to the application of this ancient technique can be found under "Dolphin De-Hypnosis" at DolphinOlogy.org.

How do you let go of the reactions and dramas that keep you circulating in less-than

BLISS CONSCIOUSNESS?

---

[12] Reverse hypnosis and then using internal sonar to feel your feelings and cry it out until laughter. "De"-hypnosis since you are already walking around in a trance.

8. DREAM-SHARING VILLAGE

DOLPHIN COMMUNITY AND LUCID DREAMS
The God Dolphins worship is their imagination.

They celebrate imagination by sharing dreams when they wake, and telling stories when they gather.

Their songs are the dreamt echoes of downloads from whales, who, according to *Star Trek*, are the historians, of the universe.

DOLPHIN DREAM-SHARING
So with any pod of dolphins, mornings are for dream-sharing. Dolphins wake and share the stories of the night and how they created worlds. For when Dolphins dream, they are aware while they are dreaming. They are AWAKE.

The dream is a participatory exercise between memories that are resolving towards healing, and the conscious control of the Dolphin to create new possibilities with the experimental images it creates to explore the dreamscape.

What are the qualities of the DOLPHIN you would want to worship?

✓ humor / Splashing
✗ how to be funny, Dolphin
 = tell the truth
 that is hidden
 (about yourself)

HUMAN DREAMS

For humans, ultimately, a dream is a karmic seed: a past action that creates guilt, longing, push-pull.

But the dream is meant to help liberate, so your inner Dolphin can be extracted beyond the High Council, back to the source of one light.

What are the
KARMIC SEEDS
you would like
to be liberated from?

Have you ever sat in a Dolphin dream-share circle?

WHAT DID YOU DREAM?
This works like the SENOI Tribe of Malaysia, who share the dream in the morning, then hear back from the tribe as if it were the others' dream... *"If that were my dream, it would feel like I was telling myself..."*

93

YOU ARE A POET - NO PHD REQUIRED

Of course, Dolphins know that all thought forms and reality arise out of the same ocean, so they know all the characters in the dream are themselves. Analyzing the dream doesn't require human books; it only requires a sense of metaphor... of poetry. OMD *(Oh My Dolphin)* - a chance to throw down some poetry! Here it comes:

I'm the dreamer -
I'm the dream -
The sea, the Seer
And what is seemed... and seen to be
Blossoming and falling and being reborn
Until these thoughts
This endless game is worn
And a dream yogi I become
To let the thought forms and desire
Melt back into the ocean
Into the **bardo** *between death and rebirth*
Thank you for blessing me
That I may recognize
The sky beyond the clouds
The silence beyond the claps of thunder
The base of all
Where wonder and suffering
melt into love
And our liberation
Benefits all those striving to
rise above birth, drama, sickness and death

- Wake Breathe Love

THANK YOU, MASTERS, FOR OUR BUDDHA-DOLPHIN NATURE

So the dream is shared. Then it is acted out, while the pod-member stops during moments of grasping, aversion, and fascination, does reality checks (looking at his palms, trying to put hands through objects, trying to fly, looking at entries and exits, then back again to see if they change; looking at clocks to see if the time has changed, but start with the palms, it's easier – see *Chapter 9: Dolphin Practices.*)

RE-DREAMING

The dreamer practices re-dreaming with awareness that it's a dream - much like we go over moments in our heads... *"I could've said such and so"*, *"Would he/she still love me if I...?"* Imagine we freed up our second guesses in the village dream-share?

The SENOI culture was neurosis- and crime-free, according to the anthropologist Kilton Stewart.

A dreamer would even bring a gift to his neighbor if he wronged her in a dream.

Dolphins play like this all day, don't you sing-feel? Dolphins and yogis living in dreamtime by the beach.

Join us at DolphinOlogy.org and maybe become part of a new-old culture.

HUMAN COMMUNITY

So, just like the SENOI tribe of Malaysia, the Ancient Egyptians, the Tibetan Dream Yogis, The Bushmen and others, one of the oldest cultures still existing seems to be the Aboriginals of Australia. Would it make sense that a culture with 50,000 years of history knows something about how to handle our passage through this life?

Despite Western development challenging these original Holders Of Truth (hotties), they live, and lived, in the dreamtime, where the entire life was ruled by the interconnectedness of dreams shared.

From my Wiki search, I learned the land was planted and social structures organized according to the dreams of the tribe. Songs, relationships, agriculture all moved forward through an interconnectedness with Nature and visions shared through the dream.

Storytelling is the communal recounting and practice of dream lucidity, where we share our stories of the night and our tribe members act them out as if they were their own, so we can witness and become aware of our own patterns, and ultimately wake up with each other.

Music as well, just like Dolphin clicks and whistles, is a story form meant to be a heart expression to build awareness and to pray through song, pray for the ability to be present and awake to the lucidity of the moment.

YOUR KID A BRAND ROBOT?
Videogames and movies have replaced rites of passage like the dream-share. They bond kids and adults to brands and products instead of each other's hero's journey.

MOVE TO THE VILLAGE?!
DolphinOlogy.org has a list of off-the-grid villages that already are sprouting up! For example, Damanhur.com in Italy, Pachamama in Costa Rica,...

Pack a light bag for the tropics. Papaya is cheap from the trees. I'll say it again so we can find each other: DolphinOlogy.org.

Perhaps: If you can't leave until tomorrow, turn off the computer, cancel the trip to the movies (this from a former film director and now each others' mother,) upside down the newspapers and do a Dream-Share – do you really want to see-feel anything less than love in your field of possibilities? Especially your unconscious possibilities?

With the separation that the moneymakers created with those box prisons ("apartments") – we have lost our ability to celebrate tribally, while preparing for the most powerful life (an awake death.)

JUICY RITUAL OR ROBOT TV?

Okay, this writer is starting to flow now: run to the Dream-Sharing Village, reclaim the heart, for that juicy sharing, that hot ritual around the campfire, where the dance and play and lascivious worship is the felt-sense that we are looking at ourselves in bodies playing a game.

The inner smile glow that enraptures our senses is the reason the Balinese are always tooth-grinned on their island paradise, where they even celebrate Engine Day once a week by putting incense and flowers on boat engines for the engine spirits to be recognized. Imagine if this was done in your life to waken you to the dream.

OLD-AGE SEXY

Might old age be fun, as we slip into the eternal dream with hard-chiseled sexy steel muscles of imagination.

What better "gym body" to share with your eternal lover than off-the-planet, conscious, notebook-style dying with your soul mate on an epic journey towards a same vision. A vision of an afterlife on a water-planet where you two can make Dolphin love in clean, anti-gravity Dolphin-air all twelve sun-moon day-nights long, or past all cyclic existence into the One Love Blue Sky; The Buddha Field.

WHOSE HAND?

So next time you dance to music, look at your hand swaying, like the Sufis doing their whirling dervish dance, and ask, "*Whose?*" Is it the dancer's or the dreamer's hand?

Or pick up the phone and share a story of your dreams with your family. Or better yet, build a village. We want to visit.

THE VILLAGE

This is where we are at, a crossroads where civilization is both becoming more built up and falling apart as the economy changes and fault lines continue to unpeel along seaboards, bringing people back into contact with their porpoise: to prepare for change - the ultimate change, eventually.

Does it make sense that blending into community; losing identity to the service of others and the Earth and elements from which we came, will be more graceful than losing identity, home, family, sex and sexuality all in one sudden transition we experience at the last breath?

So be a Dolphin: give a smile, send a healing vibration; splash someone.

9. DOLPHIN PRACTICES

What is your
PRACTICE
of being vulnerable?

- Cry openly
- clear feelings
- give the victory
  to the one who
  needs it.

Soon we will be able to communicate with the oldest dream-tribe: Dolphins. Until then, the channel of their practice feels like this:

HOW TO BE A LUCID DOLPHIN DREAMER

Unlike a Dolphin body, the human body goes into paralysis before sleep to prevent acting out dreams. The brain pings the body to see if it's asleep yet - this is the urge to roll over. Once the fidgeting before sleep stops, the brain knows to shut the body down.

If we consciously avoid the urge to roll over or fidget, and we keep our eyes fixed on a solid point, we get sent to sleep very quickly. If we don't submit to the urge to roll over, we will remain conscious and stay aware of the sleep paralysis settling over our bodies, and we can stay awake into the dream state.

To bypass falling asleep while going into sleep paralysis:

1. Lying on your back, don't toss, turn or move.

2. Fix your eyes on a single point.

3. Notice as the body goes into paralysis by listening for the "BUZZZ" that will start humming in your ears.

4. Focus on your breathing.

5. As the images of dreamscape arise, be aware of the tricks to remain lucid:

   a. Spin to keep your attention moving and not fall into a Compulsive Game.

b. Look at your hands to refer to yourself as a character in a Voluntary Game.

c. Test reality by looking for opportunities to fly, to walk through walls, to have special powers and then refer to your hands or spin.

A NOTE ON SPINNING
Lucid dream teachers Carlos Castaneda and Stephen LaBerge suggest the palms will swirl when you see them in a dream.

When one looks to the palms during the day, there is a witnessing aspect that one may realize he is the witness of the body.

For me, simply looking at the palms stabilizes lucidity. Moving the body from fixed attention also works as we tend to get caught in the fascination of forms and experiences.

Practice this witnessing technique of looking at the palms during the day, then if you look at your palms while in a dream, you may find yourself becoming aware you are dreaming - and this can help you become less reactive, even during the day, as you realize you are in a long dream (not so long.)

So spin the body and watch for the hands. In Dolphin Dream Yoga (see *MORNING POD PRACTICE* below) this is a natural progression of awareness and movement, which includes the breath, *prana* and love.

LUCID DREAMING CAUTION

When studying lucid dreaming, realize it's all a path back to union with the Clear Light – beyond the story machine. This awareness is part of *Rigpa*[13] in Tibetan Buddhism.

While there are many techniques within these pages to become awake in dreams and life and "death," the truth is that these are all mental gymnastics. The ancient yogis had it down, so let's follow their lead when we're ready for it. It must be assumed, through one path or another, after a few or a million lifetimes, it's only a question of when, not if, we will be ready.

Let's begin with end in mind. Since it's a scientific fact that Dolphins see and transmit fractal holography (geometric sonar is the language they emit from the front cavity of their skulls,) they are therefore seeing and sending very similar images to what an enlightened being sees in Tibetan meditation. In complete darkness, in the Tao tradition, the same images arise after only a few days of light being absent.

Cool? Right! But let's not get too excited, because to have awe even at miracles is making them into a story, and makes them seem other than natural. Miracles are natural, when one steps away from seeking them outside of the sales/advertising world, which replaces them on this earth dream, with self-importance miracles (texting and selfies,) and sensual brainwashing (advertising and food.) And the story machine

---

[13] In *Dzogchen* teaching, *Rigpa* is the Clear Light of original mind-space. The non-dual singularity beyond story, the web of infinite nothingness from which all manifests and is intrinsically linked. It's not possible to describe in the brief experience this writer has experienced, except to say that when it is reached, it creates a loss of identity and one can come out of the state, my teachers say, hours, minutes, days later with no concept of time. It is the "base" of all *Dzogchen* meditation.

is what we are dissolving for those who hope to get to unity with the Divine.

Vibe what this dolphin is sonar-ing to you? God, i mean Good! So, the point here is the point of light in the heart. It's not a metaphor but an actuality that in every yoga-based tradition, the mind stills until it filters perception through the heart. And then one is seeing through a filter of light, which actually exists as the nerves (*Nadis* in Hindu, *Lung* in Tibetan) are cleared by breathing exercises (which is what dolphins and whales do all day, holding and diving.) When the *Nadis* or channels of a human body are clear, they collect *prana/chi/* the Holy Ghost in the heart center. This is provable by laying still without moving a muscle as one falls asleep. Check in on any lucid dream or out-of-body experience (OBE) group and you'll find that it's a known phenomenon that an electric current begins upon sleep paralysis (the beginning of sleep where the body freezes itself so dreams don't get acted out,) and moves towards the center. So, here is where we will jump to some advanced stuff before getting back to easy *DolphinOlogy*!

EXAMPLE OF A LUCID DREAM
A recent post from my astral projectors Facebook group offered a good reminder, in which the traveler was awake in a dream and a beautiful girl wanted to make love to him. He said out loud, "*Clarity now, if there's gonna be any union, it will be with the Divine.*"

And as such, for that moment, he bypassed infinite physically suffering lifetimes in favor of permanent bliss. But how to have this level of awesome awareness the Ancient yogi way?

THIS AUTHOR KNOWS NOTHING
This author knows nothing. NOTHING! Vibe this: every time a new level is reached, the old one is left in the last dream; stepping stones to the next level. So our reality checks and

DolphinOlogy handshake practices, which appear in this book as techniques to enjoy others and have a wake-up reminder in lucid dreams, are silly self-invented extractions, which pale in comparison with the secrets revealed by the true yogis.

If one could simply see Christ beyond the eye of every person they meet, knowing it is their mind creating the person standing in front of them, and all of the stage of the world, that would be enlightenment. However, along the way are many teachings in this book that have made progress possible at different levels of awareness. So choose your vehicle.

For example, though the body can be trained, very few people have the physical capacity to even begin the *"bepping"* practice, requiring a full lotus fold of the legs while in the air. So see what appeals to you throughout the book and please forgive any omissions or self-indulgent misdirections.

Some practices shared in this book come simply from the genius of the Internet. For example, just came back from Bhutan with Buddhist scholar Ian Baker, and Karma Rinpoche, a highly trained Tibetan yogi, but neither of them knew about the technique I'm about to give you from sacred-texts.com, which these fingers found from dancing around the web. It simply worked once as a self-experiment, and was powerful enough to give me the desire to make a self-reminder and share with you in my public notepad, this book.

THE INTERNET SACRED TEXT OF THE 6 YOGAS OF NAROPA

If one is going to be awake in the most subtle and last test of the day, and probably lifetime, then a map is needed... a map with signals would be better. So after reading the above "caution" and seeing below why and how tonal sounding into the heart is important, and grasping what the meaning of the central channel is, consider these words:

Aaaa, nu, da, ra...

These four symbolic sounds stationed at the left of the heart at 3 o'clock, at 6 o'clock, 9 o'clock and 12 o'clock are symbolic places of focus as the dream goes from:

Closed eyes, to the body switching to autonomic breathing, to imagery starting up, to full story coming on (WHICH IS WHERE WE GET LOST.)

So instead of giving you the breakdown of the esoteric text - this is a note to self: examine this suggestion from *The Six Yogas of Naropa* as translated by Marpa, a student of Sage Naropa:

Breakdown your dream stages by yourself. Allocate them to places around the heart as suggested above, *and finally land in the heart center when you make your awareness last into the story stage, and envision the* Hung *symbol.*

The Hung symbol, silently chanted with a long extended vowel: "*Huuuuung,*" is the lineage-old destroyer of *samsara.* And perhaps it is vibratory Sanskrit, or not, but either way, since enlightened beings have used it, tune in to the frequency.

Samsara is the illusion of life being anything other than a dream. *Samsara* presents continual ego correction[14] specifically tailored to the seer, giving the opportunity to unite with God, the cosmos, etc.

---

[14] Ego correction would be life reminders that we are here for each other's liberation rather than our usual sense that we exist for individual advancement. The opposite of ego is selfless service. "I" is such a lonely concept.

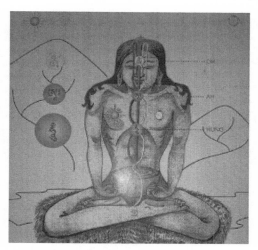

Why use the symbols and sounds from Tibetan Buddhism, or any other faith?

Registration papers! They come from Masters who have achieved the goal before, so why not tune in?

HOT BODIES OF TIBETAN YOGIS

Upon finishing this book, it was learned that the Tibetan yogis who practice heating their bodies while naked in the snow are actually lucid dream masters. By pushing life force into the central channel – which is like a tube going up the middle front of the spine – their body heats up.

By generating and concentrating this heat and, furthermore, generating wisdom *prana*[15] instead of simple heat, then consciousness gets pushed to the heart, and mind fluctuations move to the still point where the light of the Divine resides.

It makes sense that at the same time that the mind stills, the yin/yang, the 0 and 1 (in computer jargon), the male and female energies of the left and right channels, that create the

---

[15] Wisdom *prana:* being able to lose the sense of the self, so one is in the arms of the Divine.

nostrils switching flow every ninety minutes, all get balanced, and the Divine Light or Holy Spirit or *kundalini* gets activated, bandwidth now moving in the center channel towards the heart and connecting to the "motherboard," allowing lucidity, and eventually a place beyond dreams, the Clear Light, to arise naturally. Naturally arising means it's physically locked in as a function of *prana* flowing in the central channel.

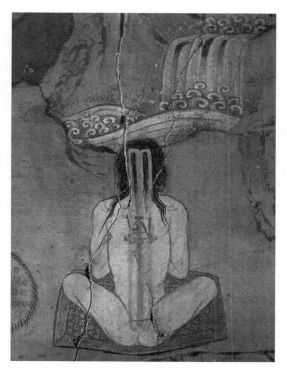

When the central channel is open, the Divine electricity, that is otherwise normally scattered, has a clear channel to the heart center, awake!

113

We're talking another world here. But then again, if we are not preparing for the other side of this life, then what are we doing? Dreaming of another terror-filled dramatic and random re-birth, peppered with learning all over again? And misled by food and sex and useless achievements? If we are lucky enough to share what's before our very eyes right at this very moment as transcriber and reader, we must use this precious time to unite with who we truly are.

Anyone teaching lucid dreaming without discussing central channel heart *prana* activation hasn't been exposed yet to Tibetan practices, or is holding back...

TUM-MO

Tum-mo is the Tibetan heat yoga practice described in *The Six Yogas of Narop*a. All of the practices flow from the ability to generate warmth in the bitter cold. The end test *of Tum-mo* practice is the monk's ability to dry sheets of cotton with his or her naked body. Oh, and the sheets are first dipped into a hole cut into an iced-over lake!

Tum-mo is a Tibetan word made up of two components. *Tum* is a masculine term that means "fierce," and *mo* is a feminine component related to "women." You can translate it as "fierce woman;" sometimes it's translated as, "She who terrifies the ego." *Tum-mo* is also a name for the Divine Mother; it is the name of Kundalini.

The *kunda* (short for *kundalini*: an empty vessel) makes room for the release of the Divine current.

Tum-mo activates in the forms of heat, *kundalini*, central channel control, so it involves breath retention, fierce shaking of the body to distribute the current once it's flowing, and also the practice of *Nauli*[16] which is a great digestive aid, but

---

[16] *Nauli:* the isolated contraction of the central abdomen muscle. It is then churned left to right and right to left. My Divine guru MaharajJi, who lives at 9,000 feet in the Himalayas without electricity or food, reports that when *Nauli* can be performed 108 times while breathing, combined with the practice of *Kechari* (the tongue inserted into and up the back of the throat to stimulate the "Divine Nectar" release from the pineal complex), one can then become food-free also.

used correctly it's also a 45-minute daily advanced practice to push *prana* into the central channel.

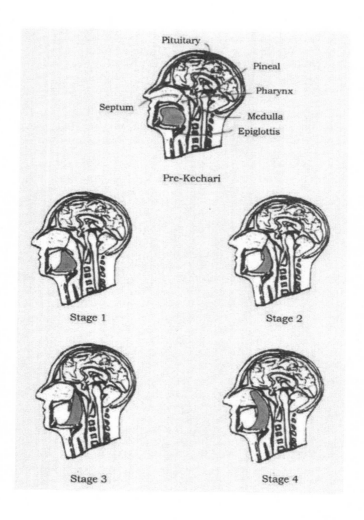

The practice of "bepping"[17] is another component of *Tum-mo*.

(CAUTION: trying this without guidance can result in the early release of *kundalini,* which can cause psychosis.)

AAAAA

Together these moves create a lasting fire symbolized by the tonal sound of *"AAAAA,"* and visualized as a column of light that is at first like a laser rising from in front of the coccyx through the top of the skull and becoming the size of the universe.

This tonal sound of *"AAAAA"* that allows one to follow *prana* into the heart during death and sleep is also visualized as the Tibetan letter "A"[18]. As one of the vibratory symbols of creation, this description of what it does and where it goes makes much clearer the notion of, "And in the beginning was the word..." (see *Chapter 12: Om Fractals, Yogananda and Master Christ Yogi.*)

So, *Tum-mo* generates the ability to fixate and become the base light of all, *Rigpa,* from which Tibetan meditative states begin.

Also called the nature of mind, this state leaves the meditator without reference to subject or object. No time and no meditator exist, and the body is forgotten. When stable, the same rigid column of Divine current keeps the body easily erect for hours or days, and allows the Divine nectar to flow

---

[17] *Bepping:* jumping up with legs into lotus position then dropping onto the tailbone.

[18] Sanskrit, as you may know, is an alphabet that forms from sound waves moving sand on a drum surface into holographic shapes. From here the Sanskrit alphabet was derived.

from the pineal complex downwards, delivering a feeling of bliss and freedom from need for food and water.

Lucid dreaming is a natural byproduct. Moreover, the Clear Light beyond dreams becomes the practice, since one can move past the story machine, just like a high dolphin or whale!

And while this is an extreme attainment from much practice in this or previous lifetimes, it must be presented here. If it calls you, you can find it in texts about *The Six Yogas of Naropa*[19].

The point is that the mental gymnastics of lucid dreaming can and should be skipped if you are ready for full enlightenment practice, because time is precious. For the first time in this short dream of "history" (what a joke that some think a few hundred thousand years of space-time is an actual history,) we can access the paths to enlightenment online and from lineages that have achieved it. So, don't forget the lineage and get your rocket ship registration before taking flight. One doesn't need a license to fly, but it helps the control tower to welcome you upon landing, yes?

---

[19] *The Six Yogas of Naropa* is available at sacred-texts.com.

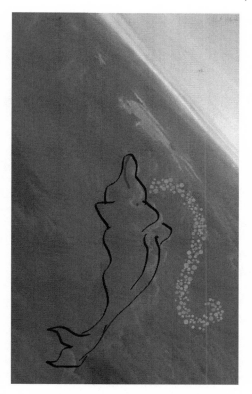

INTRO TO MORNING POD PRACTICE AND DOLPHIN DREAM YOGA

Yoga used to be (and still is) an art form to still the body, still the mind, refresh the glands and strengthen the system, in order to help the Yogi maintain equanimity under the pressure of the illusory world.

This illusory world includes the "bardos" at the time of death ("bardos" is Buddhist for the "in-between state".) This in-between state, or existing in the illusory world, includes our personal checklist of joyful accomplishing, fear and wrath, all that we are faced with in the realm of visions that occur as we lose consciousness, the different levels of dreaming consciousness that are, in a way, our nightly practice for dying.

Recently on retreat at Ligmincha International, I realized that being in anything other than a completely devotional surrounding of yoga and chanting is reason enough to check if you are in the dream, if you are being grasped by the illusory world. Simply practicing to be in a constant state of devotion or awareness expansion is reason enough to check if one is or is not in a dream state. Following is a suggested "Morning Pod Practice."

MORNING POD PRACTICE

Half an hour before sunrise – or whenever you can – with warm breathing into the heart:

1. *Temple Blessings to Self and Guru* prostrations to enter the temple (from Tibetan Bön Buddhism.)

With arms wide above the head, bring the field of infinite Dolphin Buddhas to your crown, throat and heart chakra, while humming, *"Ah, Ohm, Hung."* Feel the lights of non-dual awareness entering you from the high master Dolphin, or your choice of Guru (devotion gives that sense of sacred learning; use sacredness to fill your heart.)

Release all of your past life and concerns to the ground with a sweep of the hands to the back.

Bend to the floor and touch your forehead to the earth, thanking the oceans for not being reborn in lower realms and delivering you teachings toward liberation. Do this three times.

On the fourth, don't sweep but accept your present self and get ready for some Yoga!

2. DOLPHIN DREAM YOGA
Turning physical exercise into dream yoga.

Dolphin Dream Yoga is nothing more than a bunch of reality checks during yoga practice.

These reality checks while awake are all reminders and muscle builders to alert you to the fact that we are inside the dream of the illusory world. They are also practice for lucid dreaming when asleep.

Raise palms in the air, checking for swirling palms.

Mountain Pose with legs and bondas locked (anus and stomach held tight, the throat relaxed, crown of head reaching to the sky) - attempt to fly.

Bend to the ground; try to put the hands through the floor.

Flat back; attempt to put hands through shins.

Downward Dog, with wild legs lurched over, checking soles of the feet for swirling.

Vinyāsa through Up Dog to Down Dog...

RECAP your dream last night while in Down Dog, and look for areas you could have reality-checked, or were caught in fascination, or grasping, or aversion.

Hop up and act it out, stopping to reality check. (This will look funny, but Dolphins aren't self-conscious.)

The practice continues on like this. For more, check online, join a class, be an intuitive teacher... and don't think you need a $3,000 Yoga Alliance course in order to teach.

Dolphins always help each other without certificates, because they don't need money!

3. AFTER DOLPHIN DREAM YOGA
Use the stillness.

Following physical yoga practice, meditate for ten minutes or more, allowing thoughts to arise from the bottom of your "ocean" in a thought bubble to the surface of the still water, until no thought is left.

4. DOLPHIN GURU YOGA
Imagine your choice of Master / Masters / Guru / Deity / Symbol of Worship... imagine this delivering white light to

your crown, red light to your throat, blue light to your heart. Absorb these non-dual lights into your feeling space, and then allow your Master to dissolve into them blending into one white light which floods into your heart from the heart of your Master, who is now only a ball of light. This light pours into your heart and you dissolve into that light as well. Liberation through devotion.

It was read in some Tibetan text (probably from Tenzin Wyangal Rinpoche) that Guru Yoga is the most important practice and itself may lead to liberation.

5. CHANTING/BREATHWORK
Twenty minutes.

Use the gorgeous sounds of Snatam Kaur, Dolphin downloads, and special songs we have at DolphinOlogy.org.

6. DREAM SHARE
As described in previous chapter: *Dream-Sharing Village* – follow the example of the SENOI tribe.

7. Hugs and Yogi tea. Raw smoothies. Surf for Guru. Service to others.

DREAM TECHNIQUE FROM SUN-GAZING MASTERS

An easy dream technique from sun-gazing master Swami Suryendu Puri and his master, Paramahansa Buddhi Puri Jr.:

"When you have a dream, trace it backwards. What emotional chord needs resolving? Trace it backwards and dissolve it."

FEEL THE FUTURE: DOLPHIN LAW OF ATTRACTION

This is the coolest practice as it trains you to be non-reactive and behave like a Dolphin who only FEELS THE FUTURE when conflicted.

Can you imagine seeing nothing but places to stub your toe after you rammed it into the table? That's the old way. New Dolphin Consciousness, FEELS THE FUTURE NOW.

FEEL THE FUTURE NOW... *NATURALLY ORGANIZING AS WOW!*

That's the Law Of Attraction: where your attention goes, energy flows. So be your own Dolphin Creation Device and form new worlds: feel the earth smiling, crops growing naturally in small farming communities, GMO- and nuclear-free, people living in villages where self-importance is based on group good and sharing... Envision the happy village... living off of the land.

EMOTIONAL FREEDOM TECHNIQUE (E.F.T.) AKA "TAPPING"

If you haven't heard of E.F.T. (Emotional Freedom Technique,) then *DolphinOlogy* is pleased to offer this relief. Just as a Dolphin pulses sonar into his friends' stuck energy blockages, E.F.T. uses emotional acupressure points to do the same.

This may sound unscientific, but try it and know that you are sending attention or "Prana" from the energy points to the mind's circuits to unbind them. It works.

Following the diagram on the previous page, tap each starred pressure point seven or so times, using your middle and index finger.

Then, in any shape or form, and using your imagination to shorten the words and expand the feeling, say to yourself while tapping:

"I completely love and forgive myself, and this feeling is letting me do that."

Or: *"Thank you for allowing me this opportunity to heal; I flow love to (xyz.)"*

Or simply: *"Thank you, God."*

Or: *"Dolphin love, yes!"*

Just as dolphins send holographic[20] sound waves to each other and the Creation Device, while you are tapping, feel the

---

[20] Holography is a technique that enables a light field, which is generally the product of a light source scattered off objects, to be recorded and later reconstructed when the original light field is no longer present, due to the absence of the original objects (producing a "hologram" or "holograph".)

truth of yourself as a sacred geometric reflection of your worship, of your gratitude.

Treat the body as a world you are creating with your nurturing love. Use your inner spiritual Dolphin-Einstein to create spacious star fields of warmth-birth-galaxial-Dolphin-sonar-Love in the challenged area you are healing.

Your inner Dolphin sonar is literally creating worlds (Visit http://resonance.is for more on Einstein's unified field theory being brought to life by Dr. Nassim Harimein.)

Watch how sound waves structure water; the holographic fractal that repeats in Nature; the human that births humans; seeds that birth trees; I&I penetrate my own organs and celestial sky with this life force of love; as I&I write this and can feel the tingling in an angry-abandoned liver coming back to life.

The Tibetan mountain-Dolphins heal illness by flowing goddesses into their organs. (See *Healing with Form, Energy, And Light* by Tenzin Wyangal Rinpoche.)

The holographic fields of Buddhas in their sacred art feel just like what is described above. Again, imagination feeds love into the holographic story translator... and the Dolphin smiles.

Holography can be thought of as somewhat similar to sound recording: a sound field is created by vibrating matter, like musical instruments or vocal cords, and is encoded in such a way that it can be reproduced later, without the presence of the original vibrating matter (Per Wiki.)

SPIRITUAL PRACTICE OF THE DOLPHIN SONG

Is this reality or is this a dream?
Chant these words and you shall see.

Is this reality or is this a dream?
Breathe with me and be free

Just a dream
Into the blue as one
Oceans of the heart
I am the sun

Repeat this mantra, make it yours, and allow it to remind you to do reality checks, which will continue that awareness in dreams. The more we chant and feel into our heart, the more the moments of the day are able to be liberated from attachment and avoidance. The dream becomes recognizable.

The dream becomes the free flow of, *"Kissing the joy as it flies, living in eternity's sunrise."*

This continues into the dream state of night, as no situation will capture our fascination, terror, or compulsion, and we will move towards meditation and merging into love in dream and life.

In my experience, this practice will help you achieve lucidity within a week.

How do you practice DOLPHIN CONSCIOUSNESS?

In meditation
I watch thoughts
rise in bubbles to
the surface and pop.
Eventually, 15 minutes or so,
no more bubbles

"Now when the bardo of dreams is dawning upon me,
I will abandon the corpse-like sleep of careless ignorance,
and let my thoughts enter their natural state
without distraction;
controlling and transforming dreams in luminosity.
I will not sleep like an animal
but unify completely sleep and practice."

Excerpt from *The Tibetan Book of the Dead: the Great Liberation Through Hearing in the Bardo*

10. DOLPHINOLOGY FOR KIDS AND PARENTS

Dolphins are like kids, with the same challenges:
Super playful. Super smart. And randomly born into bodies and pods (communities of dolphins) that pose spiritual challenge.

The Big Goal
Kids are sun-powered souls born into a body to remember their way to full creativity and love. How to get back to that place where there is no conflict?

The Little Goal
It's a spiritual game. We shall see how to get out of the play of parents' childhood dramas visiting themselves and their children.

HINT: It's all so parents can relive their pasts and get the love that was not there when they were kids themselves.

And it goes on for eternity, until the path out of karma (past action) is figured out.

How to get away from drama, conflict, pain?

If parents are missing, or unschooled in the ancient practices of the mountain dolphins who meditate in caves and know how to levitate, fly to distant worlds in their minds, and process pain without inflicting it on others, their children will likely experience a lot of drama and conflict up through adulthood.

DREAM TRAINING GROUND
Souls are pulled into desire... sometimes this is as simple as two parents who need love so badly they have sex and bang: there are new fractal (repeat geometric patterns) duplicates of themselves.

It seems this painful but full-of-learning system is built to teach us we are creators. It's such a directly painful or joyful tool, that once mastered, high spiritual beings often decide to give up family life and money and seek only the source of sun power they came from, to rejoin the ability to be everywhere at once without pain and with full creative ability. The dream training ground is Earth.

UNIVERSAL CONSCIOUSNESS: LIFE IS A DREAM
Your children can enjoy a deeper understanding of what is called Universal Consciousness: complete awareness of all things at all times. A silent, all-pervading twinkling of love.

XMEN SCHOOL IN ANCIENT INDIA
In India, the elite kids are brought up learning superpowers. They *are* the iPad. They are taught meditation, dream yoga, and get downloads from beings and teachers from beyond. Instead of math and history, they are taught law and ethics. Some of these kids can speak without words, levitate or at least grow wings at will in their dreams, and get secret teachings from the Masters in the dreamscape.

Imagine you weren't raised as a cog in the wheel of the shopping machine that uses your kids to play video games and watch violence. Imagine your kid is the video game and the warrior of peace who brings teachings to the world. Teachings that it isn't children who are too sensitive, but the world at large that is not sensitive enough, and has had to arm itself with distractions to deal with just how sensitive and in pain we really are; in pain from not being raised to fulfill the superpowers that are our true Nature.

DolphinOlogy is talking to you directly if this makes sense, because your children are the new Masters; the new teachers; the truth soldiers who will create other Masters, to create a world where video games and skateboarding have been replaced by kids who lead mini-governments, which might only be one block long, but that add up and eventually change world policy. We are talking about a world where kids heal adults who have lost their way.

Imagine this trick: all kids stop talking to their parents until all war stops. Because adults aren't usually luck enough to have superpowers. Stupid-powers would end quickly.

How is this possible? Encourage your children to share their dreams. Write them down. When your heart is melted and you start sharing your own dreams, you will discover how to be the right parent for your children.

When you disagree or feel you can't control them, you might try to get violent, like all dictators do. But if you embrace training to be a Dolphin, peace will win out. Start dream-sharing and learn some techniques to wake up inside of your dreams.

Then downloads begin; your own and your child's sensitivities will become your guide. You will learn that life is not much longer than a dream, and that will help you see what really matters. You will seek counseling from your children, because it's not so easy for adults who have been trained to be part of the shopping machine. Get ready for your superpowers, because the world needs much better games to play, don't you feel-sonar?

SONAR - BOUNCING BACK SOUND TO SEE FEELINGS INSIDE OF PEOPLE

This first tool is what a dolphin does - he bounces back the sound-picture to whoever is talking to him, while seeing and being seen. Meaning Dolphins can see inside each others' bodies to see if fear or love or something in between is being held in the organs.

BEING HEARD/GETTING NEEDS MET

Children don't feel heard by parents, and parents don't feel heard by their children.

Dolphins FEEL WITH SOUND. Imagine if you always felt heard and understood when feeling frustrated... that is the effect of DOLPHIN SONAR.

So to handle yours and your children's need to be heard, you can use DOLPHIN SONAR. This is a reliable technique to create peace and harmony.

If you can model it for your children, you will be teaching them one of the most valuable communication skills they can ever learn. Soon they will give you the same respect for your needs and feelings that you are giving them.

1. Especially if your child is agitated and insisting on your attention, stop and really listen to what your child says.

2. Repeat back what they say, making sure that you fully understand:

"What you're saying is that you want to ... (go outside, be left alone,) or want me to (notice what you did, stop yelling, buy you a toy) or that you feel (sad, lonely, embarrassed.)" Ask if that is correct.

You may have misunderstood, so please allow them to correct you if you got it wrong.

3. Really feel what it feels like to have the desire or the feeling that your child just expressed. Tell yourself how you feel. (*"That feels uncomfortable, unfair, stupid."*)

4. Translate your feelings into words your child can understand informed by any insight you also picked up intuitively from really hearing and feeling his or her words. *"I can see why you want that doll, she looks like good company."* Or, *"That is something to be proud of. Good for you."* or *"That makes me feel sad too."*

5. Only after making sure you understand what your child has said, what it feels like and letting them know that you understand, offer what you think they need now. If you can't give them what they want, offer a reasonable explanation and try to find an alternative to satisfy their need. Such as, *"We can't buy the doll today. How about we play a game together?"*

SOUND WAVES GET HELP
So, now that your know how to handle momentary drama and communication, it's time to learn to use sound waves to get help. Since you are further away from your original dolphin nature than children are, you will undoubtedly say and do things that are harmful to your child's "inner dolphin," as well as your own.

SOUNDWAVES CREATE REALITY

When patterns are pushed together a lot, it creates form. In water, in sand, in nature you can see these forms. It's called sacred geometry.

When you learn to quiet the mind, you can see sacred geometry. If you practice meditation, you will be able to let programming and patterns slide away without imprinting them on your children. But silence has to be practiced.

I DO YOGA YOU DO YOGA... KIDS LOVE YOGA
See any kid watch someone do yoga, and, the kid start doing it. That's because kids know they are sacred geometry and will move into the position naturally upon seeing someone practice it.

Kids are patterns and pattern-followers who are closer to remembering they are sound creators, like dolphins, and can FEEL THEIR WAY FREE TO SILENCE AND LUCID DREAM LOVE.

Imagine using lucid dreams to try out any physical desire and learn from the Master Dreamer how to read the effect of your action before you hurt someone? Not so hard to do.

Remember, adults are patterns that have forgotten they were dolphins, that's all.

REMEMBER - WHEN THERE IS TROUBLE, SHARE YOUR DREAMS

If you have trouble talking about something, remember that it's all a dream.

Dolphins look at everything as a dream. Your children are reflecting back some part of yourself that needs love and acceptance.

And your child's parents, siblings, teachers, and friends are just dream characters all reflecting back some part of the child. There is something worthwhile to learn from everyone and everything that shows up in life. You can help your child with comfort and nurturing, and also developing the habit of finding the positive lesson from every experience, even the painful ones.

11. DOLPHIN MEDITATION

Close Your Eyes

Go Inside

Be Free

USE YOUR TONGUE
Put your tongue to the crevice of your mouth's upper palette: this completes the body's natural energy circuit.

ERECT SPINE
Sit erect with a straight spine, so you don't fall asleep, and the spinal "receiver" can flow. Put your hands in your lap. Relax the shoulders and the mouth. Relax.

POP!
Let the thoughts arise like bubbles to the surface where they pop and evaporate.

THAT'S IT.

Feel the Freedom

Feel the Calm

Feel the Oneness

Feel the Spaciousness

SPACIOUSNESS TO HEAL
That spaciousness will dissolve tension and, like a mother holding her child, you can direct the spaciousness into your body; heal the tensions which cause challenge.

Over time, you will tune into your body and your Self, and become a master at healing and making love to your kidney and liver and spleen and heart and head.

Spaciousness instead of food or shopping or gossiping or drama.

As meditation resolves one's stories:

Sarcasm is replaced with inspired hope.

Anger replaces itself with compassion.

Adversity is felt as opportunity to flip the script.

The word "challenged" is offered to replace all words of victimhood.

Words become unnecessary. Songs become paramount over words.

Chanting begins. Dolphin love spreads.

You don't need to read past this, unless your mind is cloudy...

IS YOUR MIND CLOUDY?
When you practice meditation for the first time you may find yourself sleepy, and wonder how many thoughts are in your head clouding the true You.

Practice this twice; you will want more, and realize how we are spirits caught in a mind game, seeking a way back to our connection with all.

BLISS
Practice this three times and a certain feeling of bliss and oneness will be realized, and dramas will seem like the games they are. You will feel light and a freedom to walk towards those energies that love you.

PRACTICE TWICE A DAY
Practice everyday, twice a day for twenty minutes, and you will become a constant source of your own Dolphin Consciousness, smiling gently and singing to the sea.

FREE ZONE

As the mind stills, brainwaves slow down, and like a Dolphin or Whale, you enter the free zone: that place where the mystery schools of the universe download into you.

DOLPHINS MEDITATE

Beyond the noise pollution in the waters of our mind, from what we think is entertainment, there is a loving Receiver of inter-connectedness that is waiting to reveal the truths of our journey here. All of the great Dolphins have a meditation practice; just watch them and you can feel it.

TEN-SECOND DOLPHIN CONSCIOUSNESS

Rapid Eye Movement means the brain is in Alpha, and this state can be achieved by simply looking upwards under your eyelids. If you want to connect, even for A MOMENT to Dolphin Alpha, simply take a breath, look upwards under your eyelid and feel the flutter. You have just stuck your foot in the still waters of the free zone.

147

BE A WRITER, CREATOR, LOVER

Try this before your next creative project or flirting with another Dolphin. If you've never written, GREAT, because great creators know they are the LISTENERS.

DOLPHIN ORGIES OF CREATIVITY

Dolphins slow the mind, show up the same time every day, and let the MUSE do the work. They don't edit, they, *"Take care of quantity and let the Universe take care of quality."*

Julia Cameron's book *The Artist's Way* details a great process to connect to that inner Dolphin who wants to create. Ever wonder what those pods of thousands of Dolphins are doing? Dolphin Orgy of Creativity, yet they remain with one lifetime mate. Don't try this at home; remember they are advanced beings.

Watch Dolphins in the early morning after waking from their half-sleep, cruising through the still waters, knowing they are experiencing the wave-less projection of their minds. When rough water comes, they know they are in the play of the day, making love without the attachments that were released in the dream-share and morning meditations.

DOLPHINS FEEL COMPASSION FOR CHALLENGED HUMANS

When Dolphins sadly see a human Dolphin-hunter looking in the waves off the bow of a fishing boat, they feel the human react with pride and anger (expressing as excitement since the human, who can't control his own life, can finally control a smarter fish.) Dolphins know these hunters are creating disease in their own human bodies.

The Dolphin and Whale have compassion for the human. They know, as the water stills, and the human realizes he is looking at himself, he often has less emotional need to fish, but is often still carried forward by his circuits (for unmeditated, fetus-brain humans are easily programmed for survival.)

As the water stills and the human mind stills, the human often looks past the reflection into the blue of the sky, or the depth of the ocean. He has choices.

Meditation quiets the mind and gives choices, so we are not robots conditioned by our reactivity. You may ask, *If Dolphins are so smart, why do they get caught by humans?*

Me too. Meditate. Expand Your Inner Dolphin. Donate to Ric O'Barry's Dolphin Project at DolphinOlogy.org.

DZOGCHEN[21]

Dzogchen is the name of the "highest" Tibetan spiritual path to liberation from endless cycles of birth and death (*samsara*.) *Dzogchen* means "the great completion" – completion of the soul's purpose, as in Tibetan Victory[22].

Highest appears in quotes because what is highest for one intellect may not be so for a more practical person. However, Dzogchen is the simplest, most direct path to self-realization, liberation, enlightenment, or union with what is termed God and the cosmos – beyond the play of duality.

---

[21] *Dzogchen* is the Tibetan path that existed before Buddhism. It is said to be the simplest, most profound teaching of Tibet, for when the student can be "pointed" by a teacher through introduction and confirmation to the very real experience of the "Clear Light of emptiness," then the practice of *Dzogchen* can bypass many of the Buddhist formalities of repetitious indoctrination (like the 100,000 prostrations which were 19th century additions used to bind student to teacher.)

[22] In Tibet, "Victory" means liberation from cyclic existence: life, drama, aging, disease, death.

Since the advanced *Dzogchen* yogi ultimately sees fractal geometry as one of the signs of enlightenment, and because of the concentration on staying in the "Clear Light" as one consciously slips into aware sleep beyond the dream state, *Dzogchen* feels very close to Dolphin consciousness.

Dzogchen encompasses many techniques that bypass ritual and ceremony in order to get the practitioner to the non-dual state of emptiness: no perceiver and no perceived.

If you've already died small deaths and can understand this world as emptiness-dreams-emptiness, then perhaps *Dzogchen* is ripe for your exploration.

Dzogchen is referenced here in an Islamic quote, from Ennio Nimis' book revealing the protected secrets of *Kriya* Yoga.

> "Know that there is a physical Heart in each body. There is a spiritual Heart in each Heart. There is a Secret in each spiritual Heart. There is a Hidden in each Secret, and there is a Most Hidden in each Hidden. I am in that Most Hidden."

> – *The Secret of Islam*, 274, by Henry Bayman

BEHIND THE WIZARD'S CURTAIN
There seems to be a veil, a curtain, a screen upon which the story machine forms. We can free our mind from this form-maker.

The Flight of the Garuda, a book recommended by my friend and *Dzogchen* teacher, Lama Dolma, talks about how it is a delusion to meditate – just providing a quick fix – if one can't liberate a thought the moment it comes.

What is the true benefit of this emptiness and witnessing?

Watching the internal sun – our mind's light of connectivity? ... of motherboard connectivity? ... of uni-verse projector light?

Watching the faint light this morning while waiting for story to appear, there comes the vague form of someone (my mind) saying, *"Don't snorkel too far over there to the right of the cove, past the rocks as there are skeletons..."*

Ah, story! Then "I" say, *"Hello, old friend,"* look back at the self, let this form dissolve. Then, if not writing this, I would dissolve the thought and the one doing the dissolving.

What is left after dissolving self? A blank screen. Not a "1" or a "0," the code upon which all computers (us) are built. Not a yin or yang, not an on or off switch, but the "in-between." And in that in-between, there is a moment in which the Source light starts to become brighter.

Mind generates one thought that creates form, to play with itself perhaps. And in this on-going cycle of creation, with all fading glimpses of eternity disappearing like flashes of nothingness, the concept of empty space becomes tangible.

We are this empty space, or are we these flashes? Move between these thoughts... Or is there now a very small sharp dot of light?

Indian guru Pramahansa Yogananda says we must push through this light. Lama Dolma says it's terrifying to some, but there is a way to dive into the center of this light through to the other side.

These ideas don't feel like metaphors, any more than everything in life seems to be a metaphor. Vibe us on the other side. We are here now, together.

The nature of mind revealed by *Dzogchen* is just like a dolphin's as described in this book: visions of sacred geometry, downloads from dreamtime mind treasures, and complete union with the rainbow light of the Mother. This teaching, transmitted through mind treasures, has a shortcut to enlightenment for the student who is primed. Lama Dolma shared the prediction, "Once *Dzogchen* becomes available to the common man, it will spread like wildfire."

And so we must share this simple quote from Lama Dolma, "When mind sees itself (by looking back at the self when in meditative absorption), it creates a short circuit and the dream fades, the reality dawns... It's like waking from a night dream, and everything changes."

After three years of full immersion research to escape psychosis and near organ failure, I found that this Tibetan *Dzogchen* lineage seems to reveal the highest number of track-able enlightened beings, therefore it may be the most reliable path to Unity/God consciousness.

Dzogchen's high attainment dissolves identity through visions of sacred geometry and mandalas appearing – revealing fractal holography[23] during daytime visions. For a moment, consider that the famous "flower of life" math formula which shows how everything from the curves of a sea shell to a flower to the ratio of hand to arm to body, is the same MATH OF CREATION.

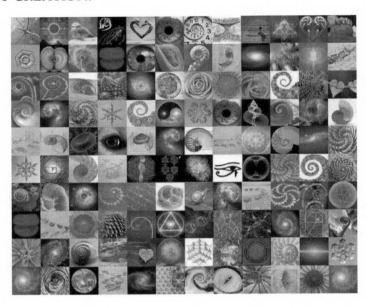

---

[23] Holography means that just like a crystal refracts images into all of its different sides, a holographic image captured on a crystal, can be shattered and each piece will contain the image of the whole. (Physicist David Boeme's metaphor: imagine a fish in a big tank and two cameras provide two views of the one fish, and from two perspectives you see two fish, when there really is one.) Or the reality of this seeming physical dream is projected onto the receiver of our consciousness, our spinal antennae, from an external united source projector, so regardless of what happens to any individual unit, or body, here, the information resolving to unite with itself, shall continue... until it does unite.

These patterns then become more and more subtle, revealing the Clear Light source. Every leaf, child, grain of sand, reveals itself to be a repeating evolving fractal of holographic intelligence. The most challenging example is easy to see if you look at children as the holographic fractal of the parent. We are fractal-makers. Self-programming artificially intelligent computers!?

So, when a terrifying Ayahuasca journey led 'me' into "psychosis" for a few months – seeing countdowns and mandalas and then losing a sense of self for a moment before sleep – "i" never realized these were enlightenment experiences.

Of course if we became awakened to the truth all at once, it would freak us out beyond life, since the final enlightenment can't even take place unless at the dropping of the body. So it makes sense that energy was shutting down my throat chakra, and i was bouncing out of bed to wake up Martha Soper, who would talk me down from not being able to breathe. While it was to the "i" to find its identity is the "piece of math" behind the story machine, this is only a step to being beyond 'form,' just as a cell is a step toward having an ego (ego='i'.)

VEHICLES TO GOD CONSCIOUSNESS

Yogananda says *Kriya* Yoga is the fastest vehicle to God consciousness, and after doing much of the *Kriya* practice, perhaps this body was prepared for some similar experiences not generated directly by an Ayahuasca plant journey.

But then again, after engaging in the *maha yoga* of a Punjabi Kundalini Ashram and Taoist darkness retreats, who's to know what is responsible for this body's healing? But there is a common denominator. And the Clear Light... the light behind the light... the light that refracts into form of all kinds... this is the common denominator. Pushing attention or

155

life force into the central channel in front of the spine, and into the heart center, which is evidently a step-up relay station to this light, this is the next step.

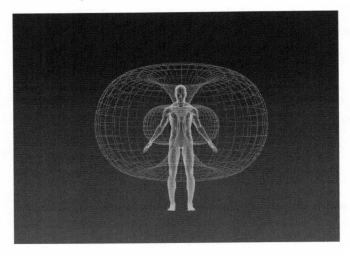

The DarkRoom Retreat reveals this after only a few days in the dark. A specific vigorous *pranayama*[24] that i won't share here, followed by a simple breath-hold, can suck one into a white tunnel in only a few minutes. But, this is done, not with the energy channeled while in *Kechari mudra*, which few people can physically accomplish anyhow, and which can send the mind into a hell realm. All of these experiences are just experiences. But to stabilize in unity consciousness, non-identity, where time ceases, the CLEAR LIGHT, what Hindus refer to as *Samadhi*... this researcher finds *Dzogchen* to have the most supportive community of practitioners with a clear path to achieve this stability.

---

[24] *Pranayama*: a breathing technique to control prana / life-force energy.

Isn't every form, star, planet, swirling consciousness, that same mind of creation duplicating itself? If we allow all of these relay points of awareness to sound the *"AAAAA,"* or *"OMMM,"* which tonally best resonates the heart center, is this not the best training to push consciousness into this necessary pathway to the Divine? Let's explore all of these questions...

To filter experience through the black hole/pure light of the heart, allows these visions to appear.

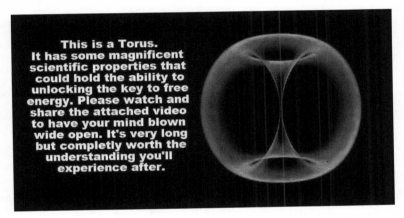

This is a Torus. It has some magnificent scientific properties that could hold the ability to unlocking the key to free energy. Please watch and share the attached video to have your mind blown wide open. It's very long but completely worth the understanding you'll experience after.

THE TOROID

The Toroidal field of energy made its debut in modern culture through the movie THRIVE. It must be assumed that ancient yogis or aliens have internally visualized and made workable this consciousness path of the breath since it is similar to guru-given breathing patterns in the Tao (microcosmic orbit,) Hindu and Shaivite[25] culture (*shiva sutra* 63.) Ah! Some power-planted good math-seeds of data to

---

[25] *Shaivism*: one of the principle forms of Hinduism.

evolve consciousness. Anyway, this has been a cool tool for creating, maintaining and playing with energy while developing an actual feeling of *prana* moving towards the heart. Master Chia said, "Now your crown is open, so you better keep circulating orbit, so you don't separate (drop body) early."

TOROIDAL MEDITATION
So while keeping it all simple, just imagine taking breath in through the crown and the anus area while a Torus spins clockwise on top and counterclockwise on bottom, and the out breath continues to push the *prana* not out of the nostrils but further into the heart center from the edges of the toroidal field up and down the spine. We are energizing our cosmic antennae. And we can see the charge of the Divine battery by pushing through the light of the third eye and merging with our internal sun. While in meditation, we are looking into the central channel, which appears as the third eye light; the light of the channel to the heart, viewed from the screen of consciousness.

To short circuit the mind by duplicating it, meaning to stop duality so we can absorb into the light that we are, the same way one would exactly mirror an angry/insane attacker, causing him to laugh and stop at his own unseen behavior... this can be taken a step further, yes? This would be to see this heart center and duplication of oneself in the eye and heart of every being or thought form that presents itself to one's awareness, whether in meditation, dreams, or the "waking" dreams we call life. Are we then in Unity consciousness, and part of the pod behind the birth of form? This and more explored as we venture forth... Let's "be here now" through this book! Yes!?

FINAL MEDITATION PRACTICE: CUTTING THROUGH
Imagine yourself meditating in front of yourself.

Realize the universe is inside of your mind. The cosmos of the eye looking back at itself leaves nothing but a blank field of consciousness... and that too is empty, as this moment will fade like another dream, as will the Witness of these words and these hands typing, and the pages of this book will dissolve back into the elements.

Behind that is mind. Emptiness. And if all is empty, then the only reasonable emotion for it all is compassion. Compassion for the self, which doesn't exist... (This process of dismantling thoughts is called "cutting through".)

THE MATRIX
And like another highest teaching, the *Zohar* – the foundational literature of Kabbalah (Jewish mysticism) – the reality we get to reveal to ourselves, through these practices, is that we are just "mind" projecting this matrix of a uni-verse. So let's just give love in every moment, regardless of what appears on the surface.

JEWISH MYSTICISM
The ultimate giver is the Creator. So if we give and give, and live to give, then we become the "Bestower" as taught in the Jewish Kabbalah. For one of the most fun paths, i have to share *Secrets of the Eternal Book* by Semion Vinokur, which reveals what has been a protected teaching for centuries. Life is revealed to be a moment-to-moment chance to correct the ego (self-serving actions.) The *Secrets* book reveals life as a perfectly computed presentation of greater and greater challenges to be compassionate and of service to others, or experience "correction," until ultimately we have no choice but to surrender to the fact that we are headed back to oneness with the Divine Giver.

HOW TO BE THE CREATOR
In the *Zohar* we get to learn how to become one of the many names of the Creator as we play up the level of losing the ego

and living to give, which ultimately reveals a physical reality of all along having given to, and having been, the One we have been serving.

Don't you agree this concept is the same in Hindu, Tibetan, and Tao as well? Behind all faiths? And all dolphin dreams? Many paths to the same ocean... where "enlightenment is our natural state." (-Lama Dolma)

12. OM FRACTALS, YOGANANDA & MASTER CHRIST YOGI

Who wants to hear ethereal sounds and be past the drama of mind, awaken inside the dream of night and day, not fear death, nor lose all the work of this life when it potentially fades like a dream?

Dolphins seem to already do this; scientifically, Dolphins have been shown to be conscious dreamers, awake inside the dream, knowing its a dream, they are always operating from the place of being Spiritual beings having a physical experience.

This is one of the most usable chapters in this book, if you stick with it.

"In the Beginning Was the Word"

Christianity: *"A-A-A-MEN"* (if you remove the men, always a good idea) = *"AMMM..."*

Buddhism: *"OMMMM..."*

Hinduism: *"AUM..."*

Kundalini Yogis have: *"Ek ONG-kar"*

Sounds form into fractals forming into Mandalas forming into physically solid matter...

163

"The Bible invariably refers to AUM as the 'Holy Ghost' or invisible life force..." (From page 314 of *Autobiography of A Yogi* by Pramahansa Yogananda.)

'The cosmic vibration AUM, the unstuck sound, the sound that contains every other sound in it.' (Paraphrasing from random Vedic sources and Paramahansa Yogananda.)

Who is closer to God than our SONAR-*OM* friends of the sea?

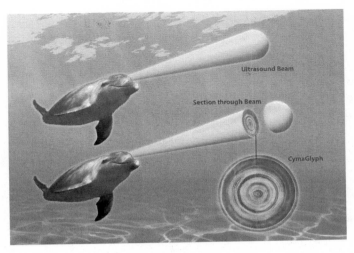

(Regarding the meaninglessness of English as compared with Dolphin sonar communication; note that "God" in Latin is *Omnipotens*[26]. Sound-sensitizing the spinal antenna and its subtle body – inches away, yet eternities away – by chanting "AUM," leads to knowing in the heart that the *Uni* - universe - is in us, and we are in *Omnipotens*...)

YOGIS AND SCIENTISTS SEE FRACTALS

Yogis, after years of meditating, see fractals forming from *Ommm* "Ajapa" yoga practice, when the universe responds with Ethereal sounds, just as Dolphins download from the "mother ship" and speak to each other using sound-feeling-images. The Cosmic sound results in vibration.

Scientists just invented the **Cymascope**, which captures sound on a water cell and it results in geometric patterns – self-repeating patterns that look like mandalas, and which are defined as fractals. Upon closer inspection, they are fractals

---

[26] One more God definition from Latin: *Paterne Omni Potencia =* Father of All Potentialities

within fractals: holograms. SOUND DNA. See cymatics.org or go to DolphinOlogy.org or Facebook.com/DolphinOlogy for links.

The Cymascope is allowing researchers at SpeakDolphin. com to build a vocabulary with dolphins! ...A visual fractal-holographic language.

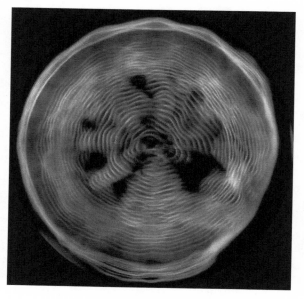

Merlin says, *"Hello"*

So, yes, sound forms fractal mandalas of energy, interconnected and holographically quantum. Sound becomes form, planes of causality: the subtle planes existing as a dream that can be awakened from. And finally, sound forms physical life.

SOUND WILL BRING US HOME
The four sounds: *"AAAA," "UUUU," "MMMM,"* and SILENCE.

The sounds of *AAA, UUU, MMM* represent the elements Earth, Water Fire, and Ether is Silence, I'd imagine...

So perhaps this book is about using our imagination to move past attachment/desire for this limited physical world, to the world of the Dolphin who is in the in-between world, closer to cosmic consciousness than individual desire.

And to recap: this desire, it is said, creates the unstruck groan of *OMMM*, which vibrates into patterns, mandalas, elements, and form...

Waves of sound create holographic fractals: repeating patterns whose fractions contain the whole;

Receivers of waves, creating simple beginnings, complex middles, and resolved ends that mirror each other; creating stories (mythological structure) within self;

And we become slave to these stories/dramas, riding on their highs and lows until we realize we can take ourselves past the story engine.

Waking, dreaming, sleeping, transcending... probably these sounds can be equated with the Holy Trinity as well as the conscious, subconscious, and the mythological field. You get the idea. Bottom line: "AUM" is the chant that texts the universe to open us to ethereal sounds and enlivens our "radio antennae" to carry us past the physical body; and Kriya Yoga contains over 100 techniques on ascending levels to enliven the spirit body.

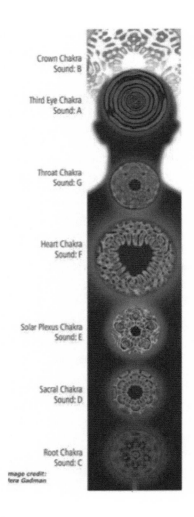

Crown Chakra
Sound: B

Third Eye Chakra
Sound: A

Throat Chakra
Sound: G

Heart Chakra
Sound: F

Solar Plexus Chakra
Sound: E

Sacral Chakra
Sound: D

Root Chakra
Sound: C

Image credit:
Tera Gadman

OMMM... OMMM...

You can use this visual reference when you place *Om* into your chakras. Chant these words and you shall see why not only Dolphins and Whales sing to each other, and GOD, but why the High Yogis experience ethereal sounds when their

Chakras (energy centers) become opened. They literally tune back into the Source of creation.

Much can be written about the types of sounds heard, but better to get it from Wiki. The true reference, from a MASTER, is Kriya Yoga[27], as discussed in the spellbinding #1 book on my shelf, *Autobiography of a Yogi*. Paramahansa Yogananda, my guru, will teach you the technique for listening to the sounds of *"Ommm"* echoed in spinal breathing meditation.

This was the last gift Steve Jobs gave to his family and friends, as reported by the news... and just before his last breath, he uttered, *"Wow, WoW, WOW!"* as his last three words.

Again, *Autobiography of A Yogi*, for a heartfelt and inspiring connection with the Master Paramahansa Yogananda.

This *"OM hearing"* is called *Anahata Nada* in the ancient Vedic scriptures.

"By the correct practice of Kriya, 14 times (yes you have to download his free book for specific instructions,) *Maha Mudra twice, and Yoti Mudra Twice, 12 years of evolution of body, mind, and soul will be gained in a few minutes.* (Some sections edited out.)

"That is how the attainment of wisdom and realization which usually takes millions of years and countless lifetimes of natural evolution, can be attained in one lifetime. Kriya is an initiation into Cosmic Consciousness, or the transfer of consciousness from the body to the spirit. In order to do this, one must transfer consciousness from the senses to the spine."

---

[27] AYPsite.org is also a great reference.

Do the world a favor: go straight to Yogananda's original book, *The Essence of Kriya Yoga* (1930) which just became available online... however it probably won't have the same kind of romantic homecoming impact without reading his autobiography. Ahhh, eBooks! Perfect.

CULTIVATING CHRIST CONSCIOUSNESS

Pink dolphins, black and white spinner dolphins, orcas, all swimming back to the mind of the great Mother....

If there is a mother ship or perhaps a motherboard that resets consciousness, then it's fair to say that what we call Christ Consciousness supports that re-setting in human terms.

Two of my teachers who qualify as masters, Maharaji Buddh Puri, who lives in the Himalayan mountains wearing only a single piece of cloth, and Pramahansa Yogananda, who departed this dream in 1952 and is considered Ascended, both wrote books interpreting the yogic metaphors of Master Christ's biblically recorded teachings.

Master Mantak Chia, who will be introduced to you in the next chapter, constantly refers to this consciousness as the Universal Intelligence.

One of the biblical interpretations is the yogic practice of *Kechari Mudra*[28] - related in the Bible, however cryptically, as Christ saying at the Last Supper, "You shall never know what I drink."

MaharajJi, who performs *Kechari Mudra,* suggests that Master Jesus may have been referring to the *Kechari* practice of inserting the tongue behind the uvula at the back of the throat so that it goes up past the nasal pharynx, eventually piercing the double bone under the pineal complex. It takes 12 years to master this practice to achieve self-stimulation of the pineal/pituitary gland by the tongue to release a bliss-inducing "Divine nectar," which allows one to meditate for days and weeks without food or water.

---

[28] *Mudra*: a brain-linking physical gesture.

Regardless, the power of uniting with the holographically-aware Savior bandwidth of Master Christ took a personal turn that must be shared out of the deepest respect and humility to everyone about everything:

Days after a plant medicine trip (ayahuasca), I was experiencing a mind-spinning melt down that felt like a sleep-deprived, suicide-inducing psychotic computer crash. Through the grace of the Creator I recalled an instruction from a friend (who had rescued me from burning electricity surging through my body) to say, "*I take all my fears and pull them into the heart of Christ Consciousness.*"

In a split second, immediately after saying this, the feelings were sucked into a hole in my heart, now Master Christ's heart, and I blurted out, "*I get it! I have nothing to fear.*"

It was like a computer "re-start" for mind and soul. Words can't do justice to the next two years of seeking to completely surrender to the Master.

So there is a book and online course that must be shared with you, noble reader of greatest compassion, that may cultivate this Christ Consciousness in you, called *A Course in Miracles*. This typing fool has been captivated by the extremely Buddhist-like exercises in *A Course in Miracles*, which states, in true dolphin-like form, that one will eventually see a rim of light around people - the holographic field of God (a similar attainment is talked about in Buddhism.)

Miracles don't deserve awe, **says** *A Course in Miracles. They are our purpose on earth. To heal each other through forgiveness.*

Meaning: forgiving others and self for separating from the One. And by requesting the "mother ship" to lead the healing and choose what "miracle" should be performed in individual daily forgiveness opportunities, which arise at ascending levels for our "correction" back to the One Mind, then the Grand Operation Designer can obviously compress or bypass time and space to heal. Time exists until forgiveness is complete. Wow!

As a service to the Mother, I thank you. May a younger me, who is you, find this work earlier and not waste a precious second of practice.

And Dolphins, with that smile, must be the last stop of consciousness in Earth flesh form – except that we have a precious human body to ascend, with a full range of emotions to forgive. So shouldn't we use it now?! And leave the programming of the illusory sales world behind?

By the way, in his *Kriya Yoga* book, a Swami I love referred to books like *Dolphinology* as the foolish work of an "aggregating author." Meaning true enlightenment that can be shared requires initiation and final accomplishment. Agreed, but this heart had no choice but to share what has given him hope. Many paths but one ocean.

Visit acim.org for the very brief daily lessons from *A Course in Miracles.* And if not already mentioned, a must-read for its poetic beauty, and a feeling of being beyond the prophets of the prophecies is the Bible through the eyes of Paramahansa Yogananda called: *The Second Coming of Christ: The Resurrection Within You.*

Enlightenment is when forgiveness replaces judgment.

When forgiveness of others, and of situations and objects, is spontaneously the first reaction rather than what once would have been judgment – on big things, little things, any little thing – this is when time stops. This is the purpose of time on earth. To forgive the images that we ourselves created to experience separation from the One. Forgive everything during all moments of awareness and expand to become like the most forgiving of all: the Creator.

If you like this, try chanting with a guttural sound into your heart center, this Buddhist version, while emanating light rays from the heart into the heart of all others: *"Om mani padme hung."*

Oh sound of creation, blossom the jeweled lotus (my heart), and destroy the illusion of *samsara*.

DolphinOlogy

13. ADVANCED DOLPHINOLOGY: DARKNESS RETREAT

Advanced DolphinOlogy, otherwise known as *Endless Cosmic Orgasm,* is collected notes to this typist-self on how to *wake up* to full brain-spiritual potential, through the coolest teachings found while traveling the world.

During the last 20 years or so, it's been a full-time job overcoming abandonment, insanity, and then a near-death psychedelic plant-induced psychosis. So, as you can imagine, this was a motivated search (LOL.)

I had some cool resources, having produced "THE CURE IS..." with a few *NY Times* bestselling authors, and having gotten email help from Deepak Chopra after my "bad trip", (we were in contact over a film idea that excited us both, about "being of the stars", funny enough.) But the sole important factor was the Grace of the Grand Operating Designer, who seems to be the only one to allow Truth to unfold, regardless of commercial polish, which is his/hers also.

Advanced DolphinOlogy will be comprised of deep explorations on my journey, such as the Darkroom Retreat. Notes from Taoist Master Mantak Chia's tao-garden.com in Chiang Mai, Thailand:

Much like Vipassana, The Buddha's Silent 10-30 Day Meditations now practiced around the world, the Darkroom retreat puts us into sensory deprivation, and a flowering of internal alchemical powers. Without food, after a process to live on Prana (life-force) for a week; without light (light blooms in the darkness); and a gradual build to silence as practitioners adjust to the darkness, this allows the cosmic consciousness to unfold. Lucid Dreams, visions, sounds, and release of the soul's Karmic memories, all are the fruits of this retreat.

JUST OUT OF THE DARKNESS

Here is the enthusiastic first Facebook post directly after turning on the computer for the first time, about 24 hours after the eyes adjusted to daylight.

Just out of DARKNESS, complete total darkness for 12 days - EVERYTHING IN THE SKY IS INSIDE!!!

Not in a metaphor, in reality.

DolphinOlogy theories CONFIRMED in this ancient Tao-PhinOlogy system!

These pictures are not that far off (as visions came in many shapes and sizes, depending on people's memories, karma, and desire.)

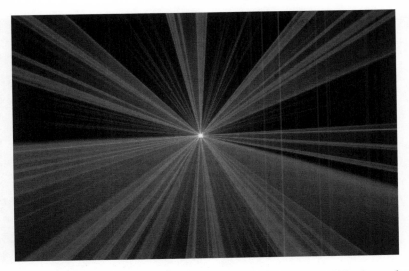

Of course the visions had a few levels... from "black and white old TV" pulsing on and off to "full HD"... details below.

Here's something cool, that "i" (ha-ha - you'll also laugh at your own identity after 12 days in the dark, or typing this book)... that "i" grabbed off the Internet.

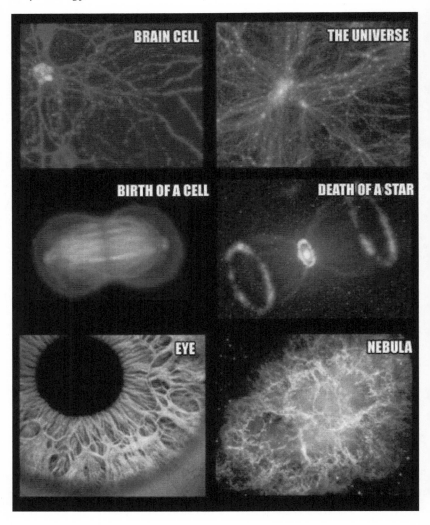

More on the macro being the micro:

human neuron

1) top left: river delta; 2) top right: human kidney; 3) bottom left: computer fractal; 4) bottom right: tree

FREE TV

While the "Free TV" offered endless visions in the dark, this group above sums up the Divine connection - note that a Google search turned up that the brain cell below is comprised of 3 neurons and a dye showing how they link, and the "Universe" is a simulation.

So, who knows where the other pictures came from, but we get the idea. Something so much bigger than us is going on; and is us, somehow. "i" bow to the Gu Ru. (Remember? Gu=Light, Ru=Dark... WOW! THE DIVINE MYSTERY) Wahe Guru.

The few people who shared (in whispers mostly, as we were supposed to be in silence, fasting) all saw full star fields and the violet light of the cosmos on and off for days... EYES OPEN OR CLOSED. This TAO system connected us with the North Star.

That is, Master Chia had us rub our hands together to activate CHI, then apply them to our occipital bone (the big one behind the head), our third eye, and our sacrum (pelvis bone.) Then he had us imagine the North Star pulsing, and LO! Did the light show begin for most!

The 4th day was so overwhelming, with a full day-night of fractals (I had a brief freak-out and Master Chia said, *"Pull your testicles, bite your lip, put your tail into the earth* (you imagine this one), *and you stop the free TV."* Laughter broke out at the "Free TV" comment, 'cause that's what was happening: Visions.

Master Chia said that his violet light turns on every time he meditates. In the new book I'm "uncovering," *Endless Cosmic Orgasm,* we get into experiments 'i' made in maintaining these connections outside of the Darkroom. This experience was so singularly powerful, "i" threw the body up and made it hug Master Chia when Darkroom was over, and was

186

through the *Endless Cosmic Orgasm* chapter outline and book cover in a few days.

WE ARE OF THE STARS

The mind (as is written in the *Tibetan Book of the Dead*) starts to show us we are made up of memories, desires, beliefs and waves of stardust... but the fractal overflow at first is so overwhelming it was stopping sleep: from art deco-like geometric patterns to Christ flames of light - always with a pulsating North Star...

I mean whoever designed our organs to take a community journey inside our bodies was, well, God-like...

We may think, the small 'i' thought to myself, that we are the identity. But actually we are housing these spirit-organs (pituitary, pineal, hypothalamus and liver, heart, spleen, kidney) who are fighting for our attention, joyfully on a ride inside our ribs and head, laughing at us, as they know we are their chauffeurs. When we get out of balance they let us know that they are in charge by taking a rest, "making us seem sick", as they heal themselves, or... sometimes they prepare to go home! They must be having a great ride, knowing that even if the body dies, they will be set free back to the cosmos.

Every day/night in the Tao DarkRoom, we smile to our organs and feel them smile back. Such a loving practice, very dolphin-like, as it brings the mind into the body. The head is opened up as a literal receiver. So, when the brain is turned off, and it doesn't have to function to survive, then the transcendent reality shines through... and truly, we learn we are of the stars...

Towards the end of completing this book, and the beginning of a new practice for me; one not expected at the beginning of this exploration; I'd like to say this Tao

DarkRoom experience gives the experiential knowledge that death is safe.

Death is safe, and perhaps navigable for those who want a more connected passage after this dream quickly fades, leaving most of humanity, it seems, in a prison of sense memories determining their fate perhaps not so randomly. LOVE FROM THE STARS.

14. DOLPHIN PREPARATION FOR DEATH

If you were a Dolphin,
WHERE
would you want
to go next?

The imaginal world of the dream is constructed with the participation of the Dolphin and kept in balance by the fact that it needs to remain awake. Thus the Dolphin, as was engineered by the High Council, is a perfect machine to build the muscle of lucidity.

DOLPHINS ARE AWARE AT DEATH?
As such, the Dolphin is also aware during death, and can incarnate into a new body. As the old body dies, and the energy which holds the lessons and memories of its past life are released, this holographic memory moves into the birth of a new Dolphin, or is extracted to the Council, or joins with the soul of creatures in need of greater consciousness, greater awareness.

EXTRACTION BACK TO THE LIGHT RAINBOW BODY
After a lifetime of play, building the muscles of dreaming-feeling-imagination, some dolphins get extracted back to the mother ship in a display of rainbow body. *(Rainbow what? It's the dissolution of the elements that create existence into their core. Like a raindrop hit by the sun will splash into a rainbow. Look around, isn't everything a miracle? Don't forget, it all ends. HOW DID WE GET HERE!? Reminder to Self: don't forget to breathe.)*

But it takes Guru yoga to make the passage safely... the same type of activity that comprises the highest of Dream Yoga teachings in Tibet, in Sikhism, and in many forms of downloaded instructions humans have channeled for eons during their meditations.

UPLOADING
It might look like this for a Dolphin, do you see-feel? : The clear light spaceship he came from requires a clear light beam of love. So Dolphins vision each other as masters, and the

elders who have achieved "rainbow body", as they feel the lights of their energy centers (equivalent to human chakras) dissolve into their heart, head, and echolocation areas.

TO MOTHER SHIP
Then they envision, in devotion to the Masters before them, their bodies dissolving into that same light and merging. This makes the mother ship not have to deal with the fear of the Dolphin in losing its fun pain-body upon extraction. Dolphin Guru Yoga. For more on this for humans, Google it.

DOLPHIN LUCIDITY IN HUMAN PREPARATIONS FOR DEATH
Just as Dolphins know their destination after extraction, or body-dropping, humans also know, on an unconscious level, when they are destined for another adventure.

For seventeen thousand years, the Tibetans (who I call mountain Dolphins) have recorded past-life memories and trained themselves to be aware while slipping into dreams, and slipping into the imaginal realm of death.

When we can be aware of the illusion that our worldly activities don't matter (unless they include the overriding awareness that old age, sickness and death are waiting,) then we can begin to be in Dolphin consciousness. To the degree that we cultivate this awareness, we can offer great compassion and forgiveness to all beings, including the animals that society will, one day, stop enslaving, torturing and eating.

In actuality, dream preparation for death, or simply being in the "vast expanse of the sky," as the Buddhist "Dolphins" call it, can allow for liberation.

For when we go into that transitory state, between life and death, according to those who have meditated in underwater caves for years, we are confronted with visions; visions of our mind, that play out in our ordinary life as the drama of our reality. Our stories of the dream, which we can't see during the day due to sensory overload, play out by showing up as our attention in daytime activities (do you click-whistle-feel it?)

This Dolphin assumes that these visions can range anywhere from the terror of our worst nightmares to the bliss of Christ or Buddha (etc.) consciousness, which is why *DolphinOlogy* encompasses all faiths, and those of less faith.

BOW TO THE ELDERS

Most revered in the Dolphin culture are the elders. For the elders have dreamt the dreams of generations: for they are almost on the other side, downloading what is next to come and what is meant to heal.

Ritual, respect and honoring elders as the living incarnation of Dolphin-Buddhas is the mainstay of the Tibetan Culture.

Imagine how this Western culture of land animals is confused by TV and brands, and all the illusions that advertising sells.

Not that it isn't fun to dance and play and sing and frolic, but isn't it more useful to be in the path of a linear trajectory, towards preparation for transition to a higher consciousness, towards liberation from the cycle of birth and Dolphin-passing? What is the point?

HOW WILL YOU USE THIS LIFE WISELY?

When it is in reverence to our Dolphin-Buddha nature, then it is truly Yogic (to yoke into oneness,) Truly Tantric (the sacred rituals to achieve oneness,) truly orgasmic, as we unleash the Kundalini-Dolphin energy in ourselves. In human Buddhist cultures, there are daily practices of video game-like preparations for travel through the bardos; so when the big one comes, the light rays and forms that come, can be recognized as the waves of an ocean that can settle back into the stillness. Like a lion looking into the water, we will recognize it as ourselves. How do you plan to use this life wisely?

This writer-Dolphin is channeling these words presently at a retreat with Rinpoche and his Holiness at Ligmincha International in Virginia. Matt, who is in a group of 20-something artists and musicians, came to this awareness unit ("awareness unit" is a more expansive way of referring to the self) and said he'd like to help with *DolphinOlogy*. He talked about his young friends that are super conscious of this illusory dream called life, and though the generation hasn't been branded, they are beyond the yoga generation and seeking the most fruitful method to prepare for what lies beyond: for the inevitable, for the homecoming.

Perhaps now is the time for Dolphin consciousness.

So let's fly in the air together, take a breath and dive deep. Deep into the vast expanse of our own sky; where the word "I", as used by my Rasta brothers and sisters, is reserved for the Most High; this body and temporary ego-identity lives to serve others and the great Mother. The One. So when you do share dreams, remember that they are all one love, one consciousness, expressing through poetry, through the emotional guidance system of our own "feeling sonar."

It feels to me like it's a small window we have in which to be blessed by the Tibetan dream yoga teachings, a small window to have the resources and awareness that miraculously allow us a chance to work on awakening and liberating.

"When parted from beloved friends, wandering alone,
my own projections' empty forms appear
may the Buddhas send out the power of their compassion
so that the bardo's terrors do not come.
When the five luminous lights of wisdom shine,
fearlessly, may I recognize myself;
when the forms of the peaceful and wrathful ones appear,
fearless and confident may I recognize the bardo.
When I suffer through the power of evil karma,
may my yidam clear away all suffering;
when the sound of dharmatä roars,
like a thousand thunders,
may it all become the sound of the six syllables."

Excerpt from *The Tibetan Book of the Dead: the Great Liberation Through Hearing in the Bardo*

RIC O'BARRY: A TALE OF LOVE

I include here the story Ric O'Barry shared with me about what transformed him from Flipper's captor to a liberator of Dolphins everywhere, as documented in the Oscar-winning movie THE COVE.

When the TV show *Flipper* stopped production, Ric's protégé dolphin was put in a tank, to live isolated and without purpose. Ric went to visit this Dolphin-actor, and she swam into his arms, looked up at him and decided it was enough with this enclosure: she expired her last breath in body and left this temporal world. A conscious death?

That moment, Ric found his life transformed - he went from Dolphin enslaver to aggressive Dolphin advocate. For example, he risks his own life to swim out to remote coves to stop Japanese butchers from taking Dolphin lives.

PHOWA: CONSCIOUS EJECTION AT DEATH

As mentioned earlier in this chapter, *mountain dolphins* are a name I give Tibetans, for like the dolphin who consciously left his body in the real life Ric O'Barry story above, Tibetans practice PHOWA: consciousness ejection at death.

Why eject your consciousness when the body is ready to stop? So, you don't appear again and think: *"Who are these parents? Why am I crying for food, love, security? Why am I here?"*

They eject their consciousness into a pre-visualized Buddha field, which dissolves into the NO-THING, just like in the TAO, just like in the still point of the Purushka in the Hindu tradition. *And just like a dolphin,* for the Tibetans who practice PHOWA, *a hole in their head opens up.* Successful practice is rewarded by the teacher inserting a grass blade into the Bindu point at the top of their skulls. Check these pics out.

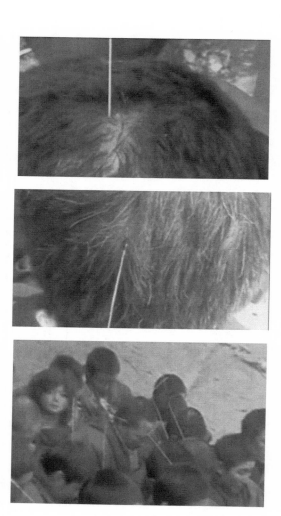

As consciousness elevates, manifestation gets quicker and quicker...

Pictured here are Ric O'Barry and his captured TV star, Flipper. The Slave-Flipper enjoyed a netted area of ocean and the company of other dolphins until the *Flipper* TV show was cancelled.

When Ric visited a month later, Flipper was now locked in a tank. As described above, Flipper swam into O'Barry's arms, looked him in the eye, let out one breath (PHOWA) and released its body, and we hope he went to the no-return Dolphin-Buddha field in the cosmos.

This was Ric's salvation: that moment he went from slave owner to liberator of the world's dolphins. His heart opened and he started giving instead of taking. He became free from the realm the Buddhists call "hungry ghost": *"More me, more I, gimme, gimme, gimme,"* and life began to bless him.

KARMA RINPOCHE

Here is how the PHOWA practice entered *DolphinOlogy* by its own tail power:

Karma Rinpoche, my PHOWA teacher and friend, asked me to clean up his English for his autobiography. The fact that he is in Bali, out of a 9-year solitude retreat consisting of 9 hours a day of meditation, and has learned pretty good English, makes this authentic and intimate sharing of his journey stand its ground.

Instead, I will teach him English so he can best share his teachings, then he can rewrite it at a later date!

Introducing Karma Rinpoche, the light-body who snaps his fingers at me during teaching, then visits the rock-n-roll hang-out after a sunset surf session, but like me, he wants to leave asap, because he only enjoys mantra… (the sounds that move you forward on the path to liberation from the cycle of suffering, aging, disease and death) instead of illusory *samsara* (the veil that convinces us this life is anything other than a quick dream that plays over and over again, in different bodies, until we get lucky, or tired, or most probably graced and get hit so hard we decide to rejoin the Divine.)

Here's a glass held high, infusing water with happiness fractals, cheering something Rinpoche represents well, at 30 years old: GENERATION LIBERATION.

Signed, his friend, Wake Breathe Love…

15. OUR TRUE NATURE

The PORPOISE of our physical bodies: *liberation of our light bodies, which existed even before the Council of Imaginations was formed.*

The message that is all around us, while we're caught in money, and celebrity, and sex, and accomplishment, is that all of these things will fade.

REALITY TV IS GETTING BORING
All the action you experience as the "world" is a TV show for "consciousness"; what the Hindu texts referred to as the play of LILA (the playground of Gods and Goddesses.) Awareness of life (and lifetimes) as a dream, filled with endless sufferings and joys is a precious window to realize that ONENESS is the only accomplishment: liberation from the cycle of birth and death and suffering.

To release karmic seeds, stories, and be free into the CLEAR LIGHT OF DREAMS (as the Tibetan Dream Yogis call it,) is the ultimate accomplishment.

FOR THE GOD IN US
Is the randomness of a dream and its location any more random than our birth to unknown parents in a random culture on an insane earth?

If this resonates with you, then consider that the entire reason for both must be, ABSOLUTELY HAS TO BE, to unite again with the creative source of both.

To wake up to the truth that we are made in God's image as a creator, and only forgiveness for separating from that Source can alleviate our self-anger and confusion, which express as "stories" and judgment. When total compassion for every moment of ego correction exists, and judgment is replaced with forgiveness, doesn't it make sense that only then can the full bandwidth of grace descend?

And when full forgiveness is our first thought; when the heart blossoms in compassion at the continual delusion of a world accomplishing anything but Divine unity; is this not when time may finally stop, and Christ Consciousness, and the Buddha field, and the seventy-two Virgins of Heaven, and the lure of fame and power also blend into a holo-fractal field of multi-pointed consciousness?

Is our degree of enlightenment not then scaled by the ability to have infinite multi-pointed consciousness?

Welcome to some possibilities...

Who are you beyond your BODY?

Life truly seems
like it delivers
continuous gifts -
to connect us with
opening the heart

FORMER PRESIDENT REAGAN

There's a story I heard from Deepak Chopra about Ronald Reagan – who had been a celebrity from his career as a movie star, who had also held the most powerful position in the world, that of U.S. President, who had a love so grand that a book was published of his poems to his wife. And at the end of his life he got Alzheimer's.

One day he was coming from therapy, holding onto a toy White House. He kept holding on to it, so his wife asked him, *"What do you got there, Ronnie?"*

Former President Reagan responded, *"I don't know. I don't know what it is, but somehow it has something to do with me."*

And this was all that was left of his memory of his own presidency. Like a baby being born into a new body, this was the karmic trace of his past.

And we all have a form of Alzheimer's, born of our karmic traces of the past: recognizing others, loving with them, fighting with them, working with them, playing with them. But the true calling is to release all these karmic traces and merge into the Oneness. So, we don't have to grasp, we don't have to avoid, we don't have to play in a reality that's going to fade away.

"The only accomplishment is liberation [from the cycle of birth and death]."

- Maharishi Mahesh Yogi

Do you realize that all of the suffering you've gone through, and walking around every day in the "grumble," and watching other people in anything less than bliss, is because we are in the in-between state, in the death state, in a hell of our own making? Just waiting to release into the knowledge that you are me, and I am you?

Because it'll be the snap of a finger until the deathbed, my friend. When the body ends, the only accomplishment will be how we release our ego. Within minutes it will be dissolved by death. Except that as of now, we may have decades to work on releasing it, instead of those few minutes.

So can we let go now and kiss our brother and sister and hug a stranger, clean their feet, take them into our arms, open our hearts, bleed our egos out into the street until we're nothing but the smile of our teeth, shining lightning bolts of love into the masses? Can you kiss me? I kiss you.

I join you in the pod; I swim with you and I play with you. Come meet me there in the ocean of our consciousness, in love, feeling, vibrating, echo-locating, sound-ing, sonar-ing, pinging... seeing through the body to the heart at play in the field of imagination.

A part of us wants to let go of even those stories of imagination, those karmic seeds, in order to see nothing but the Clear Light. Like lucid-dreaming Dolphins, we can practice letting go, and be inspired by the oldest written tradition of *Dzogchen* (to learn the 17,000 year-old practice, read *The Tibetan Yogas of Dream and Sleep* by Tenzin Wangyal Rinpoche.)

Every night these Tibetan monks practiced, in the dream state, to see between the grasping and the avoidance of dream story, to go into the Clear Light, which is our true Nature. In Tibet there are over 100,000 recorded instances of monks reaching liberation and leaving mini-rainbows over their departed bodies: a rain of enlightened souls moving back into the sky, to love the world with Clear Light.

Join me in that dream practice and we shall be love.

16. Q&A

QUESTIONS AND ANSWERS TO THIS DOLPHIN CHANNEL

I thought it would be cool to share some downloads, from opening the ocean floor to questions from friends...

If you want to ask anything, join the Dolphin pod at: DolphinOlogy.org.

QUESTION #1: *How do you let go?*

ANSWER: Just as I stop the car on the bank of a river, you have to be willing to be wherever you are. Then if you remain still, whatever it is you're holding on to can sweep away on the current of its own desire, because there is an innate organizing power to the universe.

There is a reason beyond us, beyond this Dolphin consciousness, why we are here. Which is why no matter how many times a Dolphin asks itself, *"Who am I? Why am I here? How did I get here?"* ...he is left to the three capacities of a Dolphin:

1. He has no hands, so he can't build or destroy, so he's an eternal nomad. The example to the human is, you LET GO by practicing the realization that it's not you that's building, it's your dream body in this intermediate state; it's your ego; it's something you eventually have to let go of.

So in order to prepare for a conscious death, and not be reborn into this illusory world (unless it's been so fantastic that you want to come back, in which case that's a great Dolphin game for you,) then you have to be willing to build and let go. So... have no hands (metaphorically.) That's Number one.

2. Number two to let go: A Dolphin has no language. It images pictures and feelings through echolocation. Its language is one of visuals: so don't try to evaluate another person's words and make it into your story. Because we all have a story that we tell over and over again. Our story becomes so entertaining that we start sharing this story, that confuses even us, and we share it with other people for entertainment. Then we start dancing with it over and over and over again, until our story becomes our source of entertainment that we forgot was just a story, and we believe it.

So, don't use words. If you have to send something to yourself or someone else: SEND IT AS A FEELING, DRAW IT AS A PICTURE, AIRMAIL IT AS A KISS.

And Number Three:

3. Dolphins can go into rapid eye movement, dreaming time while they're awake, so if you truly want to let go, spend no time telling stories that don't suit you, never refer to yourself or others less than positively, eliminate words like "tragedy," "bad," etc. and replace with the word "CHALLENGED."

Recognize life as a dream, put your attention on what you want, and things will begin to flower in that direction.

QUESTION #2: *I'm 65 and, with the clock ticking, I feel like I'm still sacrificing my life in devotion to my children. I love them but I want some time for myself.*

ANSWER: Maybe it's an offering to the ego version of your younger self, and by allowing and giving, you liberate from those attachments.

Be a Dolphin and travel with the pod, but let your echolocations bounce off of the expanse of the ocean. Flip out of the water no matter who is around, even if it's in the middle of your kids' performance or law school graduation. Make love in the hallway, sing outside the dorm, be wet, wild and free. The kids will thank you and have stories to tell.

After all, what business did you have in conceiving them if you can't make them laugh? Selfish human can become giving Dolphin.

To round things out, this "awareness unit" (Dolphin-I, like the Rasta, doesn't like to refer to self in any way that can lessen the experience of "I")... so: this awareness unit is asking Question number 3 to its Higher Self:

QUESTION #3: *Why did Wake have such a psychotic, suicidal reaction to his terrifying Ayahuasca ('vine of death') journey?*

ANSWER: Dolphins are used to transmitting images, knowing they only hold water weight, and can dissolve back into the ocean. But at the same time, if you let a wave hit you independent of other water, you can get slammed. Don't surf big waves alone.

From another perspective, if one is going after liberation, even the thought that one may be close is a huge ego-ic stance. And in order to be slammed back into non-ego, non-duality, perhaps the UNI VERSE (definition: *UNI* = one, *VERSE* = poetry in a song) takes those on the devoted path and allows them a reckoning. The play of the grand GURU (Sanskrit definition: GU = Light RU = dark.)

The balance of light and dark.

So, perhaps the stories of the great Dolphin masters seeing terrifying visions is the final confrontation with the grand play of light and dark of their own minds. And this awareness unit was definitely not prepared, and not guided by a master. Result: blown circuits for a year now: however the result is open channels to complete the *DolphinOlogy* download.

AFTERWORD: WORK WITH A MASTER

DolphinOlogy

A last word about serious exploration of the dreamscape and other mystical realms: <u>work with a master!</u>

This playful sharing and channeling of highest Tibetan and other teachings is intended to serve your inner work. At the same time, when one breaks through certain levels, one may pass through mortally dangerous realms and can also waste years of precious time by going it alone without the guidance of a qualified and well-chosen master.

I bow to my master Tenzin Wyangal Rinpoche (a recognized reincarnation in the Tibetan Bön lineage - see Ligmincha.org,) and several others including L. Ron Hubbard of Scientology, through his books and auditors, Guru Singh through Yogi Bajan's work (see 3ho.org.)

This writer has received life-saving relief and re-direction from all three of these Masters after an unguided Ayahuasca ("vine of death") journey, which exposed me to challenging and terrifying visions, memories, karma, etc. I was, temporarily, trapped in-between worlds.

This led to a humbling and deep reverence for *not* going it alone: advice to self.

ADVANCED DOLPHINOLOGY

In working towards liberation it's important - vital - that Master Chögyal Namkai Norbu Rinpoche be acknowledged for his statement that without transmission from a Master, liberation cannot be had through utilizing the practice of the night (dreams.)

So again, with regard to this book, it feels like this writer's dharma to share the teachings in a fun and easy-to-grasp way, so you may be turned on to the Masters, like Nomkai Norbu, whose book *Dream Yoga* provides the human source (and beyond) of these concepts that define life, death and potential non-rebirth. *DolphinOlogy* claims to know nothing but is compelled to "curate" for the Masters.

LINEAGE TEACHINGS

Just as Dolphins respect the lineage of Whales, who are senior memory masters of alien ancestry, so too do monks / swamis / Tao masters, Whales, etc. make a heart-transformer connection to the mother ship through those masters who have come before them and achieved stillness and physical attainments at death (this sign of "enlightenment" can be anything from dying from this dream in sitting position and the body shrinking to the size of a baby, to dissolution of everything but hair and nails into a "body of light", with rainbows appearing in the sky.)

So if studying for such an auspicious goal, and the only goal worth having if one begins with the end in mind, it seems to this consciousness writing here: wouldn't we want someone who can hand us help from within the Matrix they have united with?

This is lineage. An unbroken chain of teachings back to the source of an enlightened master or whale.

So, don't forget the lineage and get your rocket ship registration before taking flight. One doesn't need a license to fly, but it helps the control tower to welcome you upon landing, yes?

THE BODY ELECTRIC

Yehoshua: "We are electrical beings. Everything we do here is to support the identification with that."

This priest of Essene, a tribe of which Lord Jesus was member, is giving an intro talk into the way of life that supports electrical conductivity and the release of Shekinah, the Jewish Kabbalistic word for kundalini.

Twenty electric-bodies dressed in white at tonight's Shamanic Shabbat (Friday night celebration followed by a fast from money and technology.)

Kabbalah is the sacred mystical aspect of the Jewish tradition. Its purpose is to create spiritual rules for living, which allow for the descent of Grace (God's opening to union, sometimes felt as the electrical bliss that overtakes the body, purifying it with Holy Fire.)

That's really the entire teaching from Rabbi Cousins who is Yehoshua's teacher here in Patagonia, Arizona.

As perhaps the final chapter on paths to liberation, let me start talking less in the invented grammar that keeps people trapped reading instead of meditating, and more in:

LIBERATION: *beyond story clear light*

The way there = drop attachments, purify nerves/electrical centers/chakras and grow in stillness... and then, get this:

MEET RABBI GABRIELLE COUSINS

A new mentor, Rabbi Cousins is the founder of the Living Food movement. The natural and organic foods distributed through his organization KeHE[29] cure 70% of type-2 diabetes with freshly harvested sprouts and a living green diet.

---

[29] treeoflife.com

Shaktipat[30] from a Rabbi?

Yes. Rabbi Cousins, also a Doctor/ Psychiatrist/ Homeopath/ Hindu Priest, lived with Muktananda for 7 years. Muktananda, an Indian saint, used to wave his hand and people would go into bliss with electric/God-light blasts. The Rebbi has been similarly blessed to transmit this Shaktipat/Kundalini/Chi/Holy Ghost/Life force.

And in true dolphin form, the sacred star tetrahedron inscribed inside his 20-member temple has a crystal in the middle of it. Once one sees their first vision of sacred geometry, that's the beginning of a love affair with who we really are: something from the nothing. The Creator has used geometry, according to every faith, to form this Universe.

Check this fun animated video, it will explain what we're talking about: Spirit Science: Math of God.[31]

DROP TECHNIQUES: LEAVE ROOM FOR GRACE
So, the Rebbi's advice: drop a focus on techniques and instead let them arise spontaneously. Yoga was not something figured out to bring Enlightenment. It was a result of meditation. In fact, a Yogi was meditating and spontaneously started bending into shapes to channel energy. That's how the physical practice of yoga began.

The same way, Rebbi continues, *that all is being dreamt by G-d, and to think that we are organizing any of this with our will, continuously gets a correction from the Uni verse. As the one-song corrects our ego each moment, what is left but to SURRENDER TO GRACE.*

---

[30] *Shaktipat:* The transmission of Grace from Guru to seeker to awaken or enhance kundalini.

[31] Spirit Science: Math of God video: https://youtu.be/__bgs-DIpo8

SURRENDER

SURRENDER

SURRENDER

However, then Rebbi does add in that with enough meditation, *Shushuma* Breathing[32] will happen of its own accord. The breath going up and down the central channel as a final act of recognizing that breathing is just a dream of God who animates our breath.

And when the yogi pushes through the sleeping world of form, and can feel the cool wind of breath going up the central channel and the warm wind going down, then his normal breathing will stop. And the Yogi, in this case, the Jewish Yogi,

will be circulating the dream breath internally, as an indivisible part of all pervading G-d.

In Paramahansa Yogananda's words:

CONVERTING BREATH INTO LIFE FORCE
"When the Kriya Yogi learns to dissolve the ingoing and outgoing breath into a perception of the cool and warm currents going up and down the spine, he then feels his body as sustained by these inner currents of life force and not by their by-product of breath. He also realizes that the currents are sustained by the Word, the Divine vibratory cosmic light of prana that enters the body through the medulla. This life force becomes concentrated in and operative through the cerebral, medullary, cervical, dorsal, lumbar, sacral, and coccygeal centers that energize the body to its minutest cells,

---

32 *Shushuma*: the central energy channel that flows up and down the spine, through the main body chakras.

225

Jesus testified *that man shall not live by bread alone, but by every word that proceedeth out of the mouth of God* (Matthew 4:4.)

"This memorable passage signifies that man's body does not depend only on external sources of life force – distillations from breath, oxygen, sunshine, solids, and liquids – but also on a direct inner source of cosmic life that enters the body through the medulla, flowing then to the subtle centers in the brain and spine. In man, the medulla is spoken of as 'the mouth of God' because it is the chief opening for the Divine influx of cosmic vibratory life force, the 'word' that then flows 'out of the mouth of God' (the medulla) to the reservoir of life energy in the brain and the distributing centers in the spine.

"In successful meditation, the Kriya Yogi converts the two distinct impulses of inhalation and exhalation into two life currents, the cool prana and the warm apana, felt in the spine. He then realizes the truth of Jesus' saying—that man is not required to depend on external breath (or on 'bread' or any other outward sustenance) as a condition of bodily existence. The yogi perceives the cool and warm currents in the spine to be constantly and magnetically pulling an extra voltage of current from the omnipresent cosmic life force ever-flowing through the medulla.

"He gradually finds that these two spinal currents become converted into one life force, magnetically drawing reinforcements of prana from all the bodily cells and nerves. This strengthened life current flows upward to the point between the eyebrows and is seen as the tricolored spherical astral eye: a luminous sun, in the center of which is a blue sphere encircling a bright scintillating star. Jesus referred to this 'single' eye in the center of the forehead, and to the truth that the body is essentially formed of light, in the following words: *If therefore thine eye be single, thy whole body shall be full of light."*

Let the moment organize us.

Noble Reader/Yogic blossoming Buddha, we have come full circle, together with Rabbi Cousins leading the way to the same singing and dancing over the dinner table that this body grew up on.

So, here is a cup raised high, poured beyond full, as in the Shabbat ceremony tonight, meaning we should push ourselves past the safety realm into the dangerous but ever-watched path of unifying with G-d, and not fear joining all sages, seers, rishis, and saints who have been "crazy" from time immemorial, crazy for the Creator.

WRAPPING UP THIS BOOK
To end with the clearest last word. If we fill our life with stillness and surround ourselves with sacred geometry, then the dreams begin to fill with energy forms of sacred structure.

And if we can use this sacred geometry to get over the fear that, yes we are digital geometry, then good. It's a challenging bridge to use if the idea of dissolving the identity is scary to us.

Who wants to give up their name, and accomplishments, and feelings, and stories? Anyone who wants to not come back again and again to more story that will just fade again, like another dream.

Who is dreaming us?

GLOSSARY

Ah, Ohm, Hung: the primordial sound, whose vibratory force creates patterns and solidifies into fractals, which solidify into the elements, and then into form. Chanting these sounds resonates us back into the frequency.

Avoidance: Buddhist term meaning the attempt to flee or inability to accept a feeling or experience. When we put up our hand and say, "STOP". Anything we resist... including and especially our own emotions that constrict our organs. When this happens it's the time to flow compassion, which brings us the gift: the Present. The true Present is realizing that this is all a passing dream, that we can make subtler and softer and more refined either every incarnation (lifetime) or the now, until we merge with the dream maker.

Awareness Unit: A body, a computer with sensory input, anything that has awareness. A very detached technical way of seeing points of consciousness.

Ayahuasca ("vine of death"): a psychoactive plant concoction used by a shaman to receive plant wisdom. One of the most dangerous psychoactive substances known. It has been commercialized and sold to unwitting Westerners with good results sometimes, and sometimes psychosis or death. WARNING: Do not mess with your soul. I read somewhere even the shaman wouldn't let villagers use it; instead the shaman would drink for his tribe... until money came into play.

Bardo: a Buddhist term meaning "in-between state". We are in a death Bardo now awaiting more suffering in a next incarnation, or depending upon our collection of merit, love, compassion, and practice to dissolve the mind, perhaps liberation from birth and death. Or if you look at it the other way, freedom to be fully creative without the limit of five senses and a body.

Bepping: Jumping up with legs into lotus position then dropping onto the tailbone.

Bön Buddhism: Tibet's oldest spiritual tradition. It includes teachings and practices applicable to all parts of life, including our relationship with the elemental qualities of nature; our ethical and moral behavior; the development of love, compassion, joy and equanimity.

Chi: a Chinese term meaning life force energy, holy ghost, holy spirit, kundalini, the serpent... known many different ways, but all refer to the stored current of all-powerful spiritual energy that, when released from the base of the spine through practice or accident, can generate so much power it can either evolve the consciousness of its host to Divine consciousness, or it can drive them mad, or kill them if the electrical centers (chakras or energy centers) have not been purified.

Circuits: like computer circuits that contain programs, i.e. "if" this occurs then "xyz" will happen.

Clear Light / Clear Light of Dreams: past the dream state to the primordial "no thing" of bliss and cosmic consciousness.

De-Hypnosis aka Reverse Hypnosis: we already walk around hypnotized by survival patterns learned throughout life from those stronger than us and from social pressures, and from traumas. De-hypnosis is the process of clearing these survival moments.

Dharma: Buddhist term meaning our life purpose to serve others. Those actions that are in alignment with our greatest gifts and allow life to be lived to its highest purpose given our unique circumstance.

Dolphin-Buddha Nature: The love, joy, creativity and compassion that is natural to the Buddha and Dolphin within us.

Dolphin Consciousness: see Witness Consciousness

Dzogchen: the great completion teachings of Tibet, the "Great Perfection."

Echolocation: bouncing sound waves off of objects to see them and inside of them.

Fascination: a Buddhist term meaning locked into a state of being caught up in something and being out of balance with the present moment.

Grand Operating Design: Put the first letter Of Each Word Together and figure it out.

Grasping: a Buddhist term meaning holding onto anything. Not good in a dream, because it will overwhelm you...

Holography/Holographic: one fragment contains the whole.

Hungry Ghost: a Chinese term, similar to the Buddhist term "Preta", meaning a type of being who undergoes beyond-human suffering, particularly an extreme degree of hunger and thirst. Pretas are believed to have been false, corrupted, compulsive, deceitful, jealous or greedy people in a previous life.

Intuitive Download: a moment of pure inspiration and intuitive knowing. Downloads can be knowledge about a situation, about a person, about one's own individual soul path in the form of future awareness or past awareness (even distant path awareness, such as knowledge of past lives,) and they can even relate to areas such as technological, medical, or artistic development. Downloads tend to come entirely formed. They do not usually have the "figuring it out" feel of one's own thought process.

Karmic Seeds: Buddhist term meaning past actions that create guilt, longing and drama that will put expectation and attempted resolution into play in the future. Expectation creates results. Repetition of childhood survival tactics into adult relationships, ex. dating Daddy or Mommy.

Kundalini: a Sanskrit word meaning an indwelling spiritual energy that can be awakened at the base of the spine in order to purify the subtle system and ultimately to bestow the state of Yoga, or Divine Union. The Kundalini energy moves up the central channel of the spine to the head. Kundalini is the life force experienced as orgasm. When released by Dolphins or Yogis it's experienced as whole-body spiritual orgasm.

Kundalini Yoga: a focus on awakening kundalini energy through regular practice of meditation, breathing, chanting mantras and yoga. Called by practitioners "the yoga of awareness".

Lucidity: the ability to be aware while dreaming, and the ability to feel your dreams (be conscious) while awake.

Mantra: a Sanskrit word referring to a sound, word, or phrase that is repeated by someone who is praying or meditating. A mystical formula of invocation or incantation.

Mother: Buddhists refer to "Mother" as the eternal void from which we all came. The vast expanse of sky. The source of all.

Non-dual Awareness: a primordial, natural awareness without subject or object. Seer and seen merge into a global awareness which excludes nothing, has no center and no separation between observer and observed.

NOW: the present moment; Naturally Organized Wow.

Phowa: a Tibetan practice for consciousness ejection at the time of death.

Prana: the Sanskrit word for life force energy; in yoga, Eastern medicine, and martial arts, the term refers to a cosmic energy believed to come from the sun and connecting the elements of the universe. The universal principle of energy or force, responsible for the body's life, heat and maintenance, Prana is the sum total of all energy that is manifest in the universe.

Reverse Hypnosis: see De-Hypnosis.

R.E.M. State: Rapid Eye Movement is a stage of sleep characterized by dreaming and the rapid and random movement of the eyes. This is the stage of sleep in which the EEG brain waves operate similar to a waking state, but it is the hardest to wake up the sleeper than at any other sleep stage.

Rainbow Body: a Tibetan Buddhist term meaning the dissolution of the elements that create existence into their core. At the time of death of certain highly evolved Tibetan Masters, it is said that rainbows appear in the sky and the body of the Master disappears into radiating light, often releasing a beautiful fragrance and sometimes accompanied by beautiful celestial music.

Reality Check: a method of deducing whether one is in a dream or in real life. It usually involves an observation of some sort of sensory observation, usually visual.

Rinpoche: a Tibetan term that literally means "precious". It is used as a way of showing respect in addressing Tibetan Buddhist teachers who are recognized as reincarnated, older, respected, famous, learned and / or accomplished.

Samsāra: a Sanskrit word referring to a continuing cycle of birth, life, death and rebirth (reincarnation.) To perpetually wander, to pass through states of existence.

Seiki, Seiki Jutsu: a tradition of healing and revitalization known to have existed in the early times of Shintoism, perhaps as far back as the 8th century. It refers to the ancient Japanese shamanic ways of handling the non-subtle life force, centuries before Reiki.

Shaktipat: The transmission of Grace from Guru to seeker to awaken or enhance kundalini.

Shushuma Breathing: yogic breathing technique to generate energy flow up and down the central channel of the spine and through the main body chakras.

Sikhism: a monotheistic religion founded during the 15th century in the Punjab region of India. The central teaching in Sikhism is the belief in the concept of the oneness of God. Sikhism considers spiritual life and secular life to be intertwined.

Source: the point of origin, a generative force. In spiritual terms, "God."

Talmud: a central text of Judaism.

Terraform: The theoretical process of deliberately modifying a planet's atmosphere, temperature, surface topography or ecology to be similar to the biosphere of Earth to make it habitable by Earth-like life. To populate with flora and fauna – to birth a living eco-system.

Vinyāsa: a Sanskrit term that literally means, "to place in a specific way". There are four basic definitions: 1) the linking of body movement with breath; 2) a specific sequence of breath-synchronized movements used to transition between sustained postures; 3) setting an intention for one's personal yoga practice and taking the necessary steps toward reaching that goal; and 4) a type of yoga class.

Warm Breathing: a breathing technique used in yoga.

Witness Consciousness (the Witness, Dolphin Consciousness): a concept and a spiritual practice. To be a witness of something implies that one is watching and observing it objectively. To be witness of phenomena means that one is standing apart from the situation and not identifying with it. The practice of Witness Consciousness is meant to enable us to more clearly observe the origins of our emotions. The philosophy of Witness Consciousness teaches that our emotions are a passing phase and not our true nature.

Yogi: a Sanskrit word referring to someone who practices yoga.

A NOTE FROM WAKE BREATHE LOVE

Growing up around Florida, and brought up on *Flipper* fantasies of love, from aliens underwater, in *the* womb embrace of the sea with a perfect family of God's creatures, was a dream.

So small are we in our sense perception of one body with seven holes that "I" (in truth, an actor in God's Earth dream) could never have imagined one day realizing that this life is a dream that fades, and that the high yogis would be the true vehicle of freedom from so much grand ego and suffering amidst the apparent Godlessness of the West. These yogis simply fascinated this little boy with their nakedness in snow in the *Answer Book* (while his own body suffered in the cold winds of a 1976 New York City dream.)

Though I attempted to leave my name off *DolphinOlogy*, Wake Breathe Love (this "name" was a prayer - an intimate one) now takes public form and will be discarded, so that I may go back to "zero" without the attachment and pride that might result from carrying the "Wake Breathe Love" identity, receiving "thank yous" etc. My thanks is the gift of helping myself through your eyes, so it is I who thank you.

Thank us by sharing the free *DolphinOlogy* iBook.

* * *

This *DolphinOlogy* download and suggestions for a Dolphin Society are my own constantly evolving set of beliefs.

Keep in mind, **DolphinOlogy** *is really just a fun "brand name" to communicate some wisdom collected over time. Most of this stuff is pulled from the mother country, India, and originally inspired by the books of Deepak Chopra and Tenzin Wyangal Rinpoche (Rinpoche means recognized reincarnation of great teacher – Ligmincha.org.)*

The other stuff in here is playful imaginings, but seemed to flow into useful practices for this writer; Especially the Yoga portion and the dream-sharing collected tips. Humble prostrations to those who have lineages of Masters before them. May we all learn from each other.

The greatest way to learn and *become* the teachings is to share knowledge. Thank you for letting I&I make a humble attempt to communicate what has helped him. Use what works for you. Thank you.

I welcome your input, questions and additions at: DolphinOlogy.org.

If you enjoyed *DolphinOlogy*:

- Ric O'Barry's DOLPHIN PROJECT helps liberate Dolphins from captivity.

- Favorite causes include a sustainable DREAMSHARING VILLAGE, being created by DolphinOlogy.org.

VISIT DOLPHINOLOGY.ORG FOR MORE INFO.

What games would you create for a world and world leaders in need of far better games?

please consider making a donation:

Dream-sharing every morning, from the DolphinOlogy point of view: "*If that were my dream...*"

FREE DOLPHINOLOGY BOOKS
FOR TEACHERS TO SHARE:
Just write to: dolphinology@icloud.com

Visiting Earth Now

Master
Mantak Chia

Namkai Norbu
Rinpoche

Tenzin Wyangal
Rinpoche

Snatam Kaur

Deepak Chopra

Ric O'Barry

Karma Rinpoche

Guru Singh

Left Earth for Homecoming

Jesus Christ

Mahavatar Babaji

Pramahansa
Yogananda

Lahiri Mahsaya

Sri-Yukteswar Giri

Guru Nanak Dev

Vajra Guru
(Padmasambhava)

Gautama Buddha

Made in the USA
Middletown, DE
31 January 2023

23407781R00146